THE UNINVITED GUEST FROM THE UNREMEMBERED PAST

THE UNINVITED GUEST FROM THE UNREMEMBERED PAST

An Exploration of the
Unconscious Transmission of
Trauma across the Generations

Prophecy Coles

KARNAC

First published in 2011 by
Karnac Books Ltd
118 Finchley Road, London NW3 5HT

British Library Cataloguing in Publication Data

A C.I.P. for this book is available from the British Library

ISBN: 978 1 85575 700 4

Edited, designed and produced by The Studio Publishing Services Ltd
www.publishingservicesuk.co.uk
e-mail: studio@publishingservicesuk.co.uk

Printed in Great Britain

www.karnacbooks.com

CONTENTS

ACKNOWLEDGEMENTS

I wish to thank the following friends who have been willing to engage with this book and offer me their comments and advice: in particular, Patrick Casement, George Craig, Melanie Hart, Kirsty Hall, Hilary Rubinstein, Ann Scott, Tanya Stobbs, and Jennifer Silverstone.

I also wish to thank my patients who have been willing to allow me to write of our work together. Without them, this book would not have been possible.

Finally, and most importantly, I owe especial thanks to Walter, who has listened to my evolving ideas and read countless chapters with patient encouragement.

The cover of the book is a photograph of Betty Pinney's Doll's House, in the Museum of Childhood, Bethnall Green, London. By kind permission from V & A images/Victoria and Albert Museum. London.

In memoriam

M. A. P. 1936–2010
A. C. P. 1950–2007

Prophecy Coles trained as a psychoanalytic psychotherapist at the Lincoln Clinic and is a member of the London Centre for Psychotherapy. She is the author of numerous articles and her book, *The Importance of Sibling Relationships in Psychoanalysis*, was published by Karnac in 2003. This was followed by a book she commissioned and edited, *Sibling Relationships*, also published by Karnac.

PREFACE

Freud wrote to Binswanger on the anniversary of his daughter's death, "...we will remain inconsolable". Sophie had died in 1919 during the influenza epidemic that raged through Europe after the First World War. But Freud then had to manage another loss. Sophie's two-year-old son died two years after his mother. This led Freud to write further, "... to me this child had taken the place of all my children and other grandchildren, and since then, since Hienele's death, I don't care for my grandchildren any more, but find no joy in life any more" (quoted in Pollock, 1961, p. 353).

I am using that brief quotation from Freud's letter to Binswanger for it gives rise to the question that I am posing in this book: what legacy does grief, loss, trauma have upon the second and third generations? When Freud wrote, "I don't care for my grandchildren any more", what impact did his agonized grief have upon them?

I have an emotional interest in the idea that knowledge about ancestral history can be an important part of self-knowledge. When my brother and sister and I were quite young, our mother left us in the care of our father and went off with another man. She returned

later carrying this man's child, and we were all told that our mother
and father were reunited and that the child was theirs. We grew up
with this lie. My mother's behaviour caused all of us pain, but
behind this pain is also a theoretical question that I am asking in
this book. What impelled her to run away? What unconscious fantasies was she enacting? What part did her parents, my grandmother and grandfather, play in this complicated love affair? Was
she enacting a scene from the unremembered past of her parents or
grandparents?

On the back of all those questions runs an even more im-
ponderable one, in what way has the life I have led and the choices
I have made unconsciously carried aspects of my mother's unremembered past? Of course, I have not been able to answer these
questions directly, but some of the ideas that I explore in this
book have been impelled by a belief that we must be open to the
possibility that there may be some uninvited guests whom we need
to bring to our psychoanalytic table and ask them why they are
there.

I need to add that although I began thinking about the effect of
our ancestral past some years ago, this book is dedicated to both my
brothers, who have died while I have been writing it. Their deaths
have added another imperative to my question about the ghosts
that can haunt the nursery of life. As I witnessed them coming to
know that they were going to die, I needed more urgently than
ever to write about my sense that perhaps they went to their graves
carrying unacknowledged griefs.

The way I have structured this book is along the trajectory of a
free associative musing. There are two reasons for this structure.
The first reason is that I have found that the most liberating idea of
psychoanalysis is the concept of free association (Bollas, 2002).
When I was an anguished adolescent of sixteen, I came across
Joanna Field's *A Life of One's Own* (1934: Marion Milner assumed
the pseudonym of Joanna Field when she first published *A Life of
One's Own*). This book changed my life, for it opened a door into
my mind. I discovered that if I allowed my mind to freely associate
to whatever crossed its threshold, there were unimaginable trea-
sures and anxieties waiting to be explored. Later, when I went to
university and studied philosophy, I was drawn to thinkers who
believed that the unfurling of their own minds was the way to gain

knowledge of themselves and others, but also it was a way of understanding the history of ideas.

This leads me to the second reason for the structure of this book. The outstanding philosopher of the idea that the development of one's own mind was ineluctably part of the history of ideas was Giambattista Vico, who, in 1728, wrote his autobiography. In his book, he set out to write not an account of the events that had taken place in his life, but he was interested in exploring the history and development of his own ideas. Isaiah Berlin, commenting on Vico's contribution to philosophy has this to say,

> the notion that there can be a science of mind which the history of its development, the realisation that ideas evolve, that knowledge is not a static network of eternal, universal clear truths either Platonic or Cartesian, but a social process is traceable (indeed is in a sense identical with) the evolution of symbols—words, gestures, pictures, and their altering patterns, functions, structures and uses—this transforming vision, one of the greatest discoveries in the history of thought. [Berlin, 1979, p. 120]

This model has been my ideal throughout my intellectual life; that is to say, I have held on to the idea that, whoever we are, there is a history to what we are saying and thinking and believing that takes us beyond the here and now. So, my free associative musing is also the history of the development of my ideas as a psychoanalytic psychotherapist and, most significantly, my increasing awareness of family history across the generations.

As an example of what I mean about the development of my ideas, many years ago a patient brought me a dream in his penultimate session. In the dream, he and his girlfriend were going to his grandmother's house, for he knew that she would welcome them and give them a meal. Looking back now at that dream, I realize that I knew nothing about this man's grandmother. She had never appeared, as far as I could remember, as a significant figure in his internal world, and yet here she was, at the end of therapy. In those days, I felt myself to be far too young to be seen as grandmother, even if I was a transference figure! Imaginatively and emotionally I was out of touch with the possibility that grandparents or even great-grandparents might have a significant place in the landscape of the internal world. Time has wrought a change. I have become a grandmother and this has made me more alert to the ways in which the historical past of previous generations may shape psychic structure, for good or for ill.

I became acutely aware that my own personal idiosyncrasies must weave their way through the text of this book when, a few years ago, I attended a botanical painting course. We were taught how to observe and then paint in fine detail a botanic specimen. At the end of each day, we laid our paintings on the floor for all of us to consider. The remarkable thing about our individual paintings was that although we were all observing the same botanic specimen, the way we painted it revealed the mark of our own personality or way of seeing. Ineluctably, our own personality displayed itself in spite of our wish to give a correct account of the specimen we were painting. However ardently we may have held to the belief that we could give an accurate scientific account of what we saw, we were made aware we could never escape our personal vision of the world. I cannot escape from the emotional responses that are aroused in me, even though I have tried to walk around all sides and give an accurate description of what I believed I saw.

In the book I wrote on siblings, I suggested that if we took Freud's *Interpretation of Dreams* as the paradigm of psychoanalytic theory, we needed to face the fact that our dreams are the stuff of our theories. I put it more crisply; "psychoanalytic theory may be the theorization of autobiography" (Coles, 2003, p. 4). In the intervening years, I have not been persuaded that such an idea is doing a disservice to psychoanalysis. Only recently, Jan Abram wrote, "all psychoanalytic theories contain an autobiographical narrative . . ." (Abram, 2008, p. 1211).

So, although the structure of this book is a meditation on the ideas that have evolved over my thirty years as a psychoanalytic psychotherapist (I am indebted to Ann Scott for that idea), I want to make clear that the book's central thesis is that we must not ignore, in our psychoanalytic practice, the impact of our ancestral history, especially if our ancestors have suffered, for their anguish can return and haunt us. It is the anguished return of traumatic experience that repeats itself across the generations and affects the way the next generation is perceived.

The underlying melody of all I have written dances to the tune of Fraiberg's "Ghost in the nursery", in which she welcomes the "visitors from the unremembered past" with the idea that a new integration of their painful stories can take place (Fraiberg, 1987, p. 100).

Introduction

I wrote that the underlying melody of all that I have written in this book dances to the tune of Fraiberg's concept of the "Ghost in the nursery", though the title is taken from both Freud and Fraiberg: (1) "I hold that one should not make theories—they should arrive unexpectedly like uninvited guests, while one is busy investigating details" (Freud, 1915, pp. 73–74); (2) "In every nursery there are ghosts. They are the visitors from the unremembered past of the parents; the uninvited guests at the christening" (Fraiberg, 1987, p. 100).

These ghosts are there in every nursery, but some have the power to disrupt the wellbeing of family life. In particular, the ghosts who disturb the present are the carriers of past trauma. These ghosts are searching for a voice, and, until they are heard and recognized, they seek revenge. It is these ghosts who are the main focus of my enquiry. I have structured this book around seven chapters. In the first five, I describe different instances of trauma that may have occurred several generations ago. These traumas are of loss and abandonment, often occasioned by war, and they can impinge upon present psychological conflict, even though they may not be consciously remembered, or may have occurred outside living memory.

I begin with the idea that an unremembered sibling conflict could still be felt three generations later. I chose Aeschylus, for he seemed to suggest that conflicts and war begin with "blood feuds", that is to say, within the family. His *Oresteia* is an unfolding tragedy centred upon an unrecognized trauma. Agamemnon and his family had been the heirs to a sibling battle that had occurred between Agamemnon's father, Atreus, and his uncle, Thyestes. The unconscious message that Aeschylus seemed to understand was that trauma requires revenge unless there can be an understanding intervention.

If Aeschylus described the way in which past trauma creeps into the psychic imagination and gets enacted across the generations, the psychological details of why unconscious revenge is so powerful and destructive needed to be explored in greater detail. What is revenge trying to undo? In Chapter Two, Sophocles *Oedipus Rex* seemed to be giving a more fine-grained account of the motives for revenge. Oedipus was an unwanted child who carried his father's anger upon his shoulders. Not only was he burdened by his parents' hostility towards him, but he also suffered from being lied to about his origins. Central to understanding the tragedy that unfolds in which Oedipus kills his father and marries his mother are the two traumas he has suffered: the lie about his true origins, and the hostility that his parents visited upon him when they put him out to die. The consequence of these two traumas is that Oedipus enacts a pathological fantasy that can accompany any child who is rejected by his parents and is then lied to about his true parentage. I end the chapter with a further illustration of the idea that Oedipus is enacting a pathological fantasy that is brought about by his ancestral history and his adoption. Edward Albee in his play *The Goat*, is interpreted as exploring the Oedipal tragedy of adoption.

I place the burden of Oedipus's tragedy upon his history. His grandfather, Labdacus, had died prematurely, and, as a consequence, Laius, Oedipus's father, was disinherited from the royal throne of Thebes until his uncle died. The suffering that had been inflicted upon Oedipus's father, Laius, when he was only an infant, was an important strand in the tragedy of Oedipus. A psycho-analytic question then arises, how would we notice the presence of the past?

I took as a paradigm a quotation from Hans Loewald in which, with a beautiful lightness of touch, he said, "Those who know ghosts tell us that they long to be released from their ghost life and laid to rest as ancestors" (Loewald, 1980, p. 249). Loewald's metaphor of a ghost takes further the idea that families may be haunted by unexplored tragedies, and, in so doing, helps to ex-plain the energy that can lie behind an unacknowledged family trauma. It is as though the unmourned or unrecognized dead are literally screaming from the grave to be heard. This idea is echoed in the work of many French psychoanalysts who believe that we come into the world carrying parental expectations that are freighted with history (Abraham & Torok, 1994; Davoine & Gaudillière, 2004; Faimberg, 2005; Lacan, 1969–1970; Laplanche & Pontalis, 1968). If we ignore the unconscious messages that we carry we may be driven out of our mind, they seem to be saying.

These writers led me back to Freud and another haunting. It had been suggested that Freudian psychoanalysis has been haunted by the death of Freud's brother, Julius, when Freud was about eighteen months old (see Mitchell, 2000; Raphael-Leff, 1990). I began to wonder if we had gone back far enough. There was a sibling death in the previous generation that had not been taken into account. When Freud was about seventeen months old, his uncle Julius died. Julius was his mother's younger brother and he was twenty years old. One month after the death of Freud's uncle, Freud's brother Julius died. Freud's mother must have been depressed and withdrawn as she came to terms with her grief at the death of her brother Julius that was followed almost immediately by the death of her son. What effect did her grieving over these two deaths have upon Freud? Did the ghost of Freud's uncle Julius also haunt psychoanalytic theory; was he needing to be acknowledged and thought about?

The effect of a mother's grief and depression upon her child was brought to everyone's attention by Green's well-known paper, "The Dead Mother". He argued that if the mother is suffering a

depression at the time of the birth of her child, it can have a devas-
tating effect upon the subsequent emotional development of the
child (Green 1983). Many years after Green had written this paper,
he was interviewed by Gregorio Kohon (Kohon, 1999). In this interview, Green tells Kohon that he believes that the popularity of his
paper "The Dead Mother" is because it was based upon personal
experience of his mother withdrawing from him when he was two.
His mother became depressed at that time because Green's fourteen-year-old sister became extremely ill. However, later on in this
same interview with Kohon, he reveals that at the time of his birth,
his mother was in a state of grief because her sister, Green's aunt,
had been burned to death.

The sibling deaths of Freud's uncle and Green's aunt must have
augmented the depression of their respective mothers, but there has
been a significant silence about these deaths in the writings of
Freud and Green or any subsequent theorist. Nevertheless, these
unrecognized deaths seem to cloud the emotional language of
Freud's "death instinct" (1920g), and the chilling language of
Green's "the deathly deserted universe" (Green, 1983). Their language is carrying the weight of their mothers' grief for their lost siblings and needs to be acknowledged. I end Chapter Three with the
clinical case of Muriel, whose dead uncle, her father's brother, had
haunted three generations.

As I pursue the ghosts that can haunt our lives, I turn to grandparents. In Chapter Four, I explore the work of several psychoanalysts who have written on the negative effect that unknown or
unremembered grandparents can have upon the life of their grandchildren. In particular, there is a common acknowledgement of the
powerful legacy and influence of grandparents (Balint, 1993; Faimberg, 2005; Kestenberg & Kestenberg, 1982; Rosenfeld, 2006)). I sub-
stantiate that idea by using the clinical case of Nicholas to suggest
that he had been carrying the legacy of the traumatic death of his
grandfather, which, in turn, had affected his own father's capacity
to father Nicholas.

The ghosts of dead siblings, dead parents, and dead grandparents led me towards thinking more generally about patterns of
child-rearing. In Chapter Five, it seemed important to stop and
think more historically about the emotional response to children,

for I sensed that what had lain unrecognized within psychoanalytic theory was a history of hostility towards children. Over the past three thousand years, privileged children were frequently "farmed out" to wet nurses for the first two or three years of their life (Fildes, 1988), and if you were unwanted or illegitimate, you were put out to die if you were Oedipus, or put into an orphanage. In spite of the greater interest and understanding of the mind of a child over the past hundred and fifty years, there continues a disquieting dissociation about the effects of "farming out" children into crèches or to be brought up by others, be they nurses, nannies, or, until quite recently, wet nurses. Within psychoanalytic thinking, from Freud onwards, it has been assumed that nurses and nannies or other helpers take the role of a "second mother". One result is that these significant figures within the internal world of the child cannot be heard or thought about (Hardin, 1985). For instance, the role of the wet nurse is an unexplored topic, yet Melanie Klein had one and Freud employed one for his eldest daughter, Mathilde. I am only using the wet nurse as an example of a subtle obliteration of a very significant figure in a child's life. I turned to Shakespeare's *Romeo and Juliet* for a psychological exploration of the difficulties that confront a wet nurse and the child she had brought up. I realize that within the limits I have set myself for this book, the nurse or nanny can only be touched upon, though I hope to have shown that she is a ghost that needs to come out of the nursery and be talked about.

As I come to the end, I try to give more weight to the idea that we can be haunted by the traumatic history of past generations. I needed to show how generational trauma affects the internal structure of the psyche. I turn, in Chapter Six, to the painful history of those who survived the Holocaust. It was not until the late 1970s and early 1980s that psychoanalysts began to bring to the attention of the psychoanalytic world that the suffering of Holocaust survivors needed to be heard (Bergman & Jucovy, 1982; Kestenberg & Kestenberg, 1982; Krystal, 1978; Niederland, 1968). Until then, there had been a denial of their suffering, or a difficulty in imagining how man could survive in a world that has gone mad and in which all hope seems to have been killed. Several clinicians helped to show more clearly the way these unimaginable traumas corrode the structure of the psyche. The survivors are haunted by images of suffering in manifold ways, and their pain is communicated to their children, however protective they might have wished to be. From the therapeutic work that has been done with survivors and their children and grandchildren, we get a clearer idea that adults may unconsciously and unwittingly traumatize their infants through the anxieties that they project on to their children.

I end the book by bringing together the work of neurology and neurological research and attachment theory. The combined understanding of the brain and the psyche affords a good explanation of why the cycle of revenge continues, and brings me back to one of my original questions. What is revenge trying to do? The discoveries that have been made about the development of the brain during the first three years of life offer a way of understanding more clearly how the intersubjective experiences during the first three years of an infant's life hold the clue to mental health. Neurology not only explains the way that dysregulated or disorganized attachment damages the right side of the infant brain during these crucial early years, but it gives convincing evidence that it is the internalized relationship between mother and baby that holds the clue to well-being. Psychoanalysts and neurologists are showing how a dysfunctional relationship gets repeated down the generations, but they also hold out hope that a way of arresting the repetition is through human intervention (Fraiberg, 1987; Schore, 2002; Stolorow, 2007). It seems clear to me that if the generational cycle of abuse that follows from infantile trauma is to be alleviated, then society needs to address the overriding need to protect the next generation.

"Long is never long enough", one of my grandchildren said to me when I was telling her that next time we met we would have a longer time together. That phrase has echoed throughout the writing of this book, for, as I have come to the end of each chapter, I have sensed the truth of those words. Long is never long enough to capture an historical difficulty about where to start and where to end. We are all deeply aware of the beginnings and endings that bring us together and separate us. I realize that I have plunged into several questions in this book and hesitated between going forward or back. It has been my hope that, as I came to the end, I would find some further understanding of the questions I asked at the beginning.

CHAPTER ONE

Aeschylus and ancestral history

"... man is a historical person, the mask of his history"

(Reiff, 1963, p. 25)

The bleak landscape of generational pain and conflict and its consequences upon human moral action lies at the heart of many early Greek mythological tragedies and in particular Aeschylus's *Oresteia*. Thirty years after Marathon, Aeschylus wrote this trilogy. Scholars have pointed out that Aeschylus had a philosophical and moral interest in exploring the causes of destructive action among the many warring Greek clans, for he was called upon to help govern Athens following the Persian defeat of Marathon in 490 BC. Vellacott (1956) suggested that the trilogy was bringing dramatic form to Aeschylus's belief that a democratic political framework and a legal court were the only way of bringing peace to generations of family bloodshed. When I first wrote about the *Oresteia* (Coles, 2007), I was interested in the sibling conflict between Atreus and Thyestes as the origin of the murder of Agamemnon and Clytemenestra. More generally, I argued that Aeschylus seemed to understand that sibling relationships can hold intense emotions of

1

love and hate, and these emotions can determine the choices that people make in their life. Siblings of the same sex can find themselves in sexual conflict, such as Atreus and Thyestes, and wreak the most appalling revenge. In contrast, siblings can support each other beyond the call of loyalty such as Agamemnon going to the Trojan war to support his brother, Menelaus. Perhaps the most powerful sibling emotion is found between siblings of the opposite sex. Electra and Orestes are united in their decision to kill their mother and her lover. What I did not emphasize was that sexual conflict between siblings, as in the case of Agamemnon's father Atreus and Atreus's brother Thyestes, can have moral consequences upon the grandchildren, Electra and Orestes.

However, beyond the need for political and legal institutions, Aeschylus had the moral and psychological insight that generations of bloodshed begin within the family, and the trilogy shows that family conflict could only come to an end if there was self-knowledge and, implicitly, this involved knowledge of family history. Psychotherapists today may not have political duties or public obligations, but Greek tragedy and psychoanalysis share a common belief. They are joined in searching for a way to understand mindless intergenerational conflicts and both seem to posit that one way forward comes through telling the tale.

The trilogy itself unfolds upon a historical foundation of sibling rivalry and child murder. Atreus and his brother Thyestes quarrelled about who should inherit the throne of Argos. Thyestes had added tension to the quarrel by seducing Atreus's wife. In revenge for Thyestes' seduction of his wife Atreus murdered two of Thyestes' sons. He later served them up at a banquet and Thyestes ate them. For the Greeks, the eating of the flesh of one's family was the ultimate sacriligious act for which there could be no redress. So, Atreus achieved his wish to be ruler of Argos, for Thyestes was permanently exiled. However, Thyestes went into exile taking with him a remaining son, Aegisthus, who had survived. This background myth gives the essential structure to the Oresteian tragedy, and without that knowledge, which the Greek audience of the day would have had, the significance of Aeschylus's argument would have remained opaque.

The Oresteia is essentially a tragedy on the theme of revenge. We are led through the intricate pathways in which the wish to get even destroys even the strongest bonds of loyalty, love, and the family. The first book of the trilogy, *Agamemnon*, is like the opening of a great symphony in which different themes of filicide, regicide, and matricide are laid out, but quite central to these themes is the revenge of Aegisthus, the remaining son of Thyestes, who has a quieter but stealthy melody. He only enters *sotto voce*, as it were, at the end of the play, and we could easily forget his significance in the face of Clytemnestra's murder of Agamemnon.

To return to the opening, Atreus had two sons, Agamemnon, now King of Argos, and Menelaus, King of Sparta. They married two sisters, Clytemenestra and Helen. Helen was seduced and abducted by the Trojan, Paris, and Agamemnon felt impelled to accompany his brother Menelaus, King of Sparta, to Troy to bring back Helen. Here, we see that Aeschlyus has inverted the sibling quarrel that had beset Atreus and Thyestes, for Agamemnon, out of brotherly love, leaves Argos ungoverned to fight at the side of his brother, Menelaus. As the two brothers set out to war, Agamemnon angered the goddess Artemis, and he sacrificed his daughter Iphigenia to appease the goddess and, thus, raise the becalmed fleet. He had committed the crime of filicide.

Ten years later, the Trojans are defeated and Paris is dead. Agamemnon returns home, accompanied by his "slave" mistress Cassandra, a princess of Troy. Clytemnestra pretends to welcome Agamemnon home as a hero; however, her heart is full of revenge for Agamemnon's sacrifice of their daughter, Iphigenia. She murders him. Clytemnestra's crime of regicide is the second destructive act that adds to the unfolding drama. At this point, there is added to the acts of filicide and regicide the theme of revenge for an earlier trauma. Aegisthus, the remaining son of the banished Thyestes, had crept into Clytemnestra's bed while Agamemnon was at war. He has a quite different motive for wishing Agamemnon dead. He needs to avenge the crime that Atreus visited upon his father and he is triumphant that Clytemnestra does the work for him.

The *Agamemnon* ends, yet the audience knows that more cruelty and destruction will follow. Agamemnon's death for the sacrifice of his daughter has not expiated the crime that his father Atreus had committed. Indeed, it has augmented the crimes against the family. Clytemnestra's murder of Agamemnon is meant to expiate his crime of filicide, but, in so doing, she commits the crime of regicide, which is the worst crime of all.

Seven years later, the second play, *The Choephori*, or *The Libation Bearers*, opens. Clytemnestra and Aegisthus have ruled Argos, and created much resentment among those they have ruled. Agamemnon's surviving daughter, Electra, will have nothing to do with her mother and leads a meaningless life that is little better than that of a slave. Orestes, Agamemnon's son, returns to Thebes and is persuaded by Electra and Apollo to restore family honour by avenging the death of Agamemnon. He murders both Aegisthus and Clytemnestra.

The act of filicide in *The Agamemnon* faced Agamemnon with the anger of Artemis and his own moral responsibility for killing his daughter Iphigenia. He, in turn, is killed by his wife. In this second play, *The Libation Bearers*, Clytemnestra is faced with the moral responsibility for an act of regicide and she is killed by her son. *The Libation Bearers* ends with Orestes being pursued by the Furies. Upon his shoulders, it now seems, he carries the responsibility for all the previous crimes.

In the final play of the trilogy, *The Eumenides*, Orestes, who has gone from place to place hoping to be cleansed of the guilt of matricide, finally comes to the Temple of Apollo to ask for forgiveness. The Furies and the ghost of his mother, Clytemnestra, torment him wherever he goes. Apollo promises to make an intercession on his behalf with Athene. Orestes goes to Athens. Athene arranges a trial, which is to take place before the Furies and twelve wise men of Athens, known as the Areopagi. The Furies argue that matricide is the worst crime of all and for that Orestes should die. Orestes calls upon Apollo to put his case, and Apollo counters that regicide is a more heinous crime. When the vote is cast the result is even. Athene, the goddess of Reconciliation, is called upon to make a decision. She votes in favour of Orestes and he is acquitted of "blood guiltiness" and returns to his fatherland to rule Argos.

However, if we take the Furies as representing the most terrifying fantasy of maternal sexuality and power, Aeschylus shows that the Furies are quietened following an argument they have with Athene. They agree to change and let go of the old traditions. But what are they agreeing to? Are they agreeing to let go of the old tradition of seeking revenge for "blood feuds", or are they agreeing to "a new definition of the act of generation [that] is constituted in which no females, only males, are progenitors"? (See Simon, 1988; Vellacott, 1956.) Klein (1963) suggested that Athene is good and helpful because she has no mother and has appropriated her father, Zeus (p. 285). However Klein also maintains that Athene can tame the Eumenides (who are all women) because she promises that they will be loved by the Areopagi (who are all men) (p. 292). Her final comment on Athene is that she has

> many roles; she is the mouthpiece of Zeus and expresses his thoughts and wishes; she is a mitigated super-ego; she is also a daughter without a mother and in this way avoids the Oedipus complex. But she also has another and very fundamental function; she makes peace and balance. She expresses the hope that the Athenians will avoid internal strife, symbolically representing the avoidance of hostility within the family. [p. 297]

(I am indebted to Estelle Roith for pointing out Klein's account of the ambiguity of Athene's psychic status.)

Could it be the case that Aeschylus knows that man has dark and destructive forces within and that they have a tradition, or a meaning that can only be prevented from continuing their fertile yet destructive power through a recognition of their existence? Through Athene's discussion with the Furies, there is a veneration of the place these forces have played within the society and the psyche. It is the acceptance of the powerful part they have played in the psyche of man that can bring about a change in their role. Athene assures them they will continue to be consulted and as a result they are transformed into "the kindly ones" or the Eumenides. The fantasy of the terrifying power of maternal sexuality and fertility is shifted to allow sons to inhabit their place as generators as well.

Vellacott (1956) is surely correct when he says, "In modern times the Oresteian trilogy has rightly been accorded a place among the greatest achievements of the human mind" (p. 9). And one of these achievements must be Aeschylus's understanding of the way in which there can be no societal peace if there is a belief that it can only come about through the obliteration of the other. He also showed in dramatic form the way human behaviour is embedded in its family history, and it is this understanding that makes him so pertinent to our psychological search for reasons for human behaviour today.

Aeschlylus' depiction of the complex interweaving of human interactions and their unintended consequences makes us feel the powerful stranglehold that a neurotic circle of revenge can exert. He recreates the sense of powerlessness we can feel in the face of its necessity. At the end of the trilogy, we are left with an appreciation that for "ancient feuds" to "bleed no more" a new creative possibility has to be imagined, which involves letting go of the ancient family traumas and the desire for revenge. Aeschylus understood the difficulty of achieving such a place when the deepest passions that are aroused lie within the family. Yet, he argued that the need to seek revenge cannot underpin a well-functioning state any more than it can underpin a well-functioning family. However, he never lost sight of a profound psychological sympathy for the difficulties that prevent man from behaving in an honourable way.

Aeschylus's understanding of the conflict that can arise between family honour and the needs of a just society are not the active concerns of most therapists today. I cannot imagine any therapist with the political wish to lessen neurotic imprisonment and unhappiness so that a more just society might be achieved, though it might well be an unintended consequence. There is, however, an aspect of Aeschylus' dramatic depiction of the tension between family loyalty and individual moral behaviour that brings him close to contemporary psychoanalytic thinking on the problem of the cycle of violent action that follows upon psychic injury. Shengold uses the phrase "soul murder" to describe the effect that the destructiveness and inadequacy of parents can have upon their children: "Soul murder refers to killing the joy of life and interfering with the sense of identity of another human being". And he goes on to add, "The term 'soul murder' should be understood to indicate the actuality of external traumata—traumata that contribute to psychic pathology by influencing the basic motivating fantasies of the individual victim" (Shengold, 1988, pp. 78–80).

The phrase "soul murder" seems close to the Greek belief of a tragic fate that awaits the individual. Aeschylus's idea of a "blood feud" and Shengold's use of the concept of "the pathological compulsion to repeat traumatic events" share a common view that past traumatic events imprint themselves upon the psyche and demand an action, unconsciously, in the present. The concept of "soul murder" was first used by Judge Anselm von Feuerbach in 1832 in the case of Kasper Hauser. Daniel Paul Schreber used the phrase in his *Memoirs* (1903) and the concept was repeated in Freud (1911c) and Shengold (1988). Aeschylus was illustrating how the compulsion to repeat may go back several generations. Shengold is more concerned with the present suffering of the individual and how to help the murdered soul to recover his creativity and capacity to love in the present. He only makes passing reference to the idea that there might be a lengthy intergenerational history of "soul murder" (see Shengold, 2000, where he writes that there will be "... [a] pathological compulsion to repeat traumatic events" and "the passing down of ... abuse from one generation to the next" (p. 2)).

Another aspect of Aeschylus that makes him relevant today is that he could be seen as one of the earliest exponents of family therapy. He believed it is only the setting up of a dialogue with all the protagonists in a conflict that a more kindly place within the self and the society can be found. The newly won democratic system within Athenian society needed careful nurturing if it was to be sustained and, as Orestes confronts the Athenian court, we are made aware that a parallel process had to be found within himself before he could find peace. In both cases, the Athenian state and within Orestes himself, there is a danger that the Barbarians will break down the door and the self or the society will be flooded by destructive forces. If a reconciliation of the warring parts within the self and within the state can be brought about, then there will be a shift from fury to acceptance and kindness. It is this shift, from the need to seek revenge to a more benign acceptance of mortal and moral conflict, that allows Orestes to return to his homeland.

In contemporary terms, the individual, suffering from a neurotic cycle of repeated self-destructive action, may need to be helped to reflect upon the weight of his ancestral past that he may be carrying unconsciously. The mortal struggle with the Furies, conceived as the haunted, angry, and destructive side of the self, needs to be understood as having a past history that goes beyond the individual experience within the immediate family. This understanding might begin to free the individual from the unconscious chains of the past. The unknown script could begin to be known and the individual might no longer need to compulsively enact the tragedy.

The role of the therapist or the Areopagi, symbolizing the wise bit of the self and the external rules of society, is necessary for this change to begin to take place. But, unlike the trial of Orestes, the relief from suffering in therapy does not take place in one day. The difficulties may be extensive and the need to hold on to the Furies, or the guilt, may give rise to a lengthy negotiation, but, one hopes, in the end the voice of Athene, the goddess of Reconciliation, might be heard and her words might replace the harsh internal criticism of the Furies.

We can hear echoes of Aeschylus's account of the bleak landscape of generational pain and conflict in the following case. It concerns a woman whom I shall call Louise, who left her two young children. The pain she suffered and that she inflicted upon her children was immense, yet she felt compelled to follow her new lover. Many years later when Louise's mother died, she discovered that her mother had a sibling who was still alive. This sibling was able to tell Louise that he and her mother had been brought up in an orphanage and knew nothing about their parents. He had recently learnt that they were illegitimate and had been put into care, in early childhood, when their mother died. The loss of the "mother" seems to have been repeated unconsciously across three generations (Faimberg, 2005; Schützenberger, 1998). By that, I mean Louise abandoned her children, and this repeated, unconsciously, the unknown trauma that her mother had suffered in childhood. The result was that two sets of children were abandoned by their mothers across three generations.

The first trauma occurred when Louise's grandmother died and her mother and uncle were put into an orphanage. The second took place two generations later, when Louise left her children for her lover. It was as though Louise was searching for a lost love that in origin was the unmourned loss that her mother had experienced. Louise became the conduit of lost love and inflicted it again upon her own children as she struggled to give voice to the earlier abandonment that her mother had suffered. The destructive repetition of looking for the lost love occurred because neither Louise nor her mother had conscious knowledge of the past. Louise's mother believed she was an orphan and had no memory of her mother. If Louise's mother had been given some knowledge of her own dead mother, then Louise might have been freed from trying to find expression for her mother's loss.

Instead she enacted her mother's grief, and in doing so she inflicted a further grief upon her two children. I do not know how her children managed, but in my clinical experience, such an abandonment can leave the child with complicated unconscious fantasies of revenge upon the parent who betrayed them, yet, at the same time, there is a desperate longing for the return of the lost love. The child may have a tough battle to fight between the wish for retaliation and the acceptance of heartbreak.

A more detailed piece of clinical work illustrates the idea that the past, and in particular the traumatic past, might be echoing several generations later. It concerns Martha, who had an intractable belief that if she ate lunch she would grow fat. We had not been able to shift this conviction, nor had I been able to help her accept a lunch invitation. It was not until I began to think more historically about this belief, and asked Martha to think about her parents and grandparents, that this "phobia" began to have a meaning. Martha's maternal grandfather had died from the effect of being gassed in the First World War and was never spoken about in the family. He was a taboo subject for his wife and children and grandchildren. Martha's maternal grandmother had been left with seven children to feed and very little money. Martha's mother, who was the oldest of these seven children, was often hungry as a child and, unmindful of her own experience, she brought Martha up on a strict dietary regime that left Martha hungry as a child. In particular, Martha's mother, on a matter of principle, never cooked lunch, and this left Martha not only often hungry, but longing for her family to be like her friends and sit down to a cooked meal.

The meaning of Martha's fear of becoming fat if she ate lunch became clearer to her once she could make a link back to her mother and grandmother and dead grandfather. She could see that the strict dietary regime she had internalized from her mother hid a much more significant grief about a vanished and unmourned grandfather. It was as though the unmetabolized image of the grandfather who had died from poison gas had created a phobic image of a mouth that must be kept closed. The grandmother's refusal to talk about him seemed to have created an unconscious fantasy in her children that he must not be spoken about lest something poisonous should be taken in. Their subsequent hunger seemed to confirm this fantasy.

We have seen from the early Greek writing of Aeschylus that loss, abandonment, and the subsequent wish for revenge eats into the soul of man. These themes are also the scenes that are revisited most frequently in psychotherapy. However, if, within psychoanalytic practice, the present relationship between patient and therapist is the sole focus, there is little space to consider the way sociological and historical events in the past might have had an impact upon the individual psyche. We leave out an important part of psychic development if we do not take an interest in the history of grandparents and great-grandparents, and in particular the traumatic experiences of war, social disruption, and untimely death or abandonment.

In conclusion, Aeschylus's Oresteia is a mythological tragedy that gives psychological insight into the way family feuds can lead to the desire for revenge and civil strife. He has helped to map out the idea that family history needs to be understood and known about in order for the destructive cycle to be brought to some resolution. I used the clinical cases of Louise and Martha to explore some of the ideas that Aeschylus had set out in the *Oresteia*. However, more detailed discussion of the personal inner fantasies that accompany trauma needs to take place. In the next chapter I am going to use Sophocles' *Oedipus the King* for an exploration of the way a trauma in the previous generation can have an impact upon an individual's present conflict. It is as though Sophocles has taken up the more general psychological argument in Aeschylus and explored the way ignorance of the generational past can damage the individual psyche.

CHAPTER TWO

Sophocles and the fate of adoption

"That which is neglected escapes"

(Sophocles, 1962, line 111)

In the last chapter we saw that when Aeschylus depicted the mythological tragedy of the House of Atreus, he brought psychological insight into the way family conflict can rebound across the generations. The myth dramatized the way a blood feud can accumulate in ferocity and it highlighted the idea that an original trauma will be repeated unconsciously in the next generation if it is not remembered and spoken about. However, Aeschylus leaves his audience to put together the past history that Orestes carried and its consequences upon his present action. We know Orestes is relieved of his suffering, but it is left an open question as to whether he was aware that the blood feud began with his grandfather Atreus and his great uncle Thyestes.

It could be said that Sophocles knew that Aeschlyus had left more detailed questions about individual human motivation unexamined. It was as though Sophocles sensed that it was not a sufficient explanation of human behaviour to point back to ancient

11

feuds. And so, in *Oedipus Rex*, Sophocles presents a more personal exploration of the impact of ancestral conflict upon individual identity. Little has been made of the fact that Sophocles is suggesting that if we are to account for personal suffering, then the antecedent conditions need to be known. Oedipus's suffering was the result of the lies that were told him about his parentage. He is denied the knowledge of his true heritage, which is that his father had not wanted him and his mother colluded with his father to get rid of him. Simon (1988) made the important point that these Greek writers were reflecting the war-torn world in which they lived, and in which the abandonment of children and filicide played a part in the cultural trauma. And, as a consequence, we witness Oedipus's struggle to know himself and rule well while at the same time we see him pitted against the grain of unavoidable self-deception. On this account the tragedy in which Oedipus murders his father and marries his mother is not the enactment of a universal wish within us all, but it is the playing out of a pathological fantasy that is precipitated by the failure to tell Oedipus the truth about his ancestral history. Or, another way of putting it might be to say that he enacted the pathological fantasies of many adopted children.

To suggest that Oedipus enacted a pathological fantasy that was occasioned by his adoption, shifts the ground of the analytic shibboleth, the Oedipus Complex. But it could be said that when Freud wrote his famous letter to Fliess, on 15 October 1897, "I have found, in my own case too, being in love with my mother and jealous of my father", he is not saying that he had discovered that he wished to marry his mother and murder his father. It is true that in the same letter he writes that if his discovery is universally true for all children, then, ". . . we can understand the gripping power of *Oedipus Rex*" (Masson, 1985, p. 272). But supposing Freud really meant what he wrote, that he had discovered "being in love with my mother and jealous of my father". Does it follow that the universal desire in all children is to murder their father and marry their mother? Perhaps that desire arises as a consequence of being abandoned and lied to, or when confusion about genealogy and deception has masked the truth (Bowlby, 2007). In shifting the concept of the Oedipus complex in this way, it challenges the universality of the wish to commit parricide and incest, but, perhaps more importantly, Sophocles' *Oedipus Rex* contributes to our understanding of the destructive consequences that follow a history of family deceit.

Oedipus is the most famous case of the adopted child in the annals of the psychoanalytic literature (I am grateful to Faye Carey for her comment pointing this out). He suffers from being cast off and lied to about his original family, and we witness the blinding effect that ignorance of the past can have upon emotional develop-ment (Bowlby, 2007; Brinich, 1995; Faimberg, 2005 (who was more specific in her understanding of Oedipus's difficulties and wrote of the "Oedipal constellation", in which Laius's filicidal wishes and Jocasta's complicity were the precipitating cause of the trag-edy); Feder, 1974; Vernant & Vidal-Naquet, 1972; see also Welldon, 1992).

Oedipus came from the House of Cadmus, a family as riven by conflict, violence, and death as the House of Atreus. Cadmus, Oedipus's great-great-grandfather had founded Thebes. Two gener-ations later, Cadmus's grandson Labdacus became King of Thebes. He died when his son Laius, father of Oedipus, was only one year old. Laius, with his mother, was turned out of the royal court by his uncle. Laius wandered the world, dispossessed, angry, and father-less. As a young man and a guest at the court of King Pelops, he seduced and abducted the King's son Chrysippus. The dishonour-ing of his position as a guest at a royal court, not his sexual seduc-tion of the King's son, angered the gods, and in retaliation they prophesied that any child he had would murder him. Laius even-tually returned to rule Thebes and married his first cousin, Jocasta. He never told her of the gods' threat and instead he avoided sex with her. Jocasta, unaware of this threat, seduced Laius after she had made him drunk. Oedipus was born nine months later. Two days after his birth, Jocasta allowed herself to be persuaded by Laius that their life depended upon getting rid of Oedipus. A servant was told to put Oedipus on Mount Cithaeron to die. In-stead, the servant gave him to a shepherd, who took him to the childless King and Queen of Corinth, Polybus and Merope. Oedipus was brought up believing himself to be their child. The slow unravelling of the drama of *Oedipus the King* begins with the failure of Polybus and Merope to tell him the truth about his birth.

As in the case of the *Oresteia*, the Greeks will have been familiar with the myths surrounding the tragedy: Laius's past, his homeless and fatherless state, his homosexuality, and his failure to honour the rules of courtesy will have been part of their background knowledge. They will have been aware also that Laius tried to cheat his fate by disposing of his son, hoping that his son would die and that he would not face his own death or the crime of infanticide (Boswell, 1988; Vellacott, 1971). In other words, they will have appreciated that Laius was a complicated and cruel man, whose character had been deformed by the burdens of his life experience as well as by the weight of the history of the House of Cadmus (Devereux, 1953; Ross, 1982). This background knowledge of Laius and his subsequent fear and murderous hatred of Oedipus brings a deeper complexity to the tragedy, and as several commentators have suggested, it brings Laius and Jocasta's ambivalence towards Oedipus as an important reason for the subsequent violence (Bowlby, 2007, Brinich, 1997; Faimberg, 2005; Ross, 1982).

The play opens seventeen years after Oedipus had left Corinth in the hope of saving his adopted mother and father from the prophesied fate that he would kill his father and marry his mother. Vellacott believed Oedipus must have known that he was an unwanted baby because of his damaged feet. It was an accepted way of disposing of children, in Greek communities, to leave them to die of exposure. Vellacott (1971) and Boswell (1988) both suggest that infant exposure was an accepted way of disposing of unwanted babies in Greek communities, for it did not risk condemnation for infanticide. However, Vellacott (1971, p. 189) is equivocal as to whether foot-piercing was also commonly practised, so it is a delicate question as to whether Oedipus would have been aware from common knowledge that he was a foundling. Oedipus's sense that he was not the true child of Polybus and Merope led him to consult the Oracle and Vellacott surmises that

> When Oedipus left Delphi he regarded as probably untenable the belief that Polybus was his father. That is to say, he knew very well that to avoid Corinth would not save him from the crimes predicted; *he might meet his parents anywhere in Greece. [ibid.,* p. 93, my italics]

And so it seems that Oedipus's personal "tragedy of destiny" began when he was abandoned by his parents and it was compounded further when his adopted parents, Polybus and Merope, failed to tell him the truth about his parentage. These facts faced Oedipus with epistemological and moral difficulties. He already faced psychological doubts about whether he had been an abandoned child because of his name and his damaged feet (Boswell, 1988; Vellacott, 1971). When he consulted the oracle and was told he would kill his father and marry his mother, he was faced with the moral necessity of avoiding his supposed parents. However, the profound epistemological problem was that he did not know who he was, so how could he make the morally responsible choice?

The idea that it was Oedipus's adoption that precipitated his epistemological, moral, and psychological difficulties comes close to Watling's (1974) suggestion, in his introduction to his translation of *Oedipus the King*, that the play was about discovering the truth of Oedipus's birth. Vellacott took this idea further, and suggested that the play was a subtle working out of the way in which Oedipus failed to recognize the truth that his adopted parents were not his real parents. In this account, Oedipus "turned a blind eye" to his intuitive knowledge and began the tragic journey that led to his nemesis (Steiner, 1985). Vellacott argued that Oedipus's self-deception becomes transparent when he refused to think about the identity of the man he killed at the crossroads. He knew the man was a King, for he was in a royal carriage and accompanied by servants, but when, two days later, Oedipus came to Thebes and heard that King Laius had been killed at a crossroads two days before, he failed to make the connection with his killing of an older man at a crossroads. He continued on the road of self-deception when he married the King's widow, a woman who was old enough to be his mother. Apollo's warning had fallen on deaf ears.

So, Vellacott suggested that an understanding of Sophocles' intention is not the popular one in which Oedipus's journey is seen as the gradual unfolding of the unwelcome truth of Oedipal desire, such as Freud suggested took place in an analysis, but a much more complex exploration of the way man can turn away from knowing the truth. Oedipus suspected "his true relationship with Laius and Jocasta ever since the time of his marriage" but ignored it (1971, p. 104). Others, such as Friedman and Downey (1995), have questioned whether the incestuous wish is universal, and, from a biological–psychological angle, they suggest that aggressive fantasies between father and son are endemic, but they need to be distinguished from parricidal wishes. Loewald (1980) makes a distinction between the need to overcome the father and the pathological wish to kill him off, and Perelberg (2009) differentiates between the "dead" father and the "murdered" father. Erikson (1955) suggested that incestuous wishes and fantasies are associated with insecure bonding.

While Vellacott's understanding of the text is subtle and persuasive, Sophocles' play raises a further psychological question about the unique difficulties that an adopted child faces when he does not know his true parentage. Vellacott suggested that when Oedipus left Corinth "he knew very well that to avoid Corinth would not save him from the crimes predicted" and, furthermore, he knew "he might meet his parents anywhere in Greece" (Vellacott, 1971, p. 93). Oedipus may have suspected that Polybus and Merope were not his true parents, but how would he know who his parents were? What moral compass did he possess to help him? What would count as true knowledge? Would it have been clear to Oedipus that Laius was his father and Jocasta his mother, in spite of Apollo's warning? The enigmatic response of Apollo laid open the true vulnerability that the adopted Oedipus faced. Oedipus would only know whom his true parents were when he had murdered his father and married his mother.

This idea leads to the question as to whether Oedipus's conflict might provide insight into the difficulties that the unwanted and adopted child carries, not only as to "Who am I?", but also, unknowingly, the fantasies and actions of the birth parents that led to his adoption. Laius had been told that his son would murder him. Oedipus carried, unconsciously, the murderous hatred of his father, symbolized by his damaged feet.

The psychoanalytic literature on the adopted child points frequently to the wish to murder the father who has inflicted this "soul murder" (Colarusso, 1987; Wagonfeld & Emde, 1982), but murder is not the only desire. There is another powerful anxiety about incest. One aspect of the fear about incest is that parent and child might meet later in life with destructive consequences (Ross, 1982). Boswell (1988) has also described the historical consequences in great detail. Boswell quotes from Tertullian, in the third century,

You expose your children, in the first place, to be rescued by the
kindness of passing strangers, or abandon them to be adopted by
better parents. Naturally the memory of the cast-off relation dissi-
pates in time, and . . . in some place – at home, abroad, in a foreign
land – with lust, whose realms are universal, as companion, you
easily fix unknowingly somewhere upon a child or some other relations . . . and do not realise the encounter was incestuous. [1988,
p. 159]

Fantasies of murder, filicide, parricide, and matricide, as well as
anxieties about incest, accompany both the abandoning parents and
the abandoned child. From this reading, the moral of Sophocles'
drama is not so much the revelation of the psychological theory that
we all desire to sleep with our mother and murder our father, but
a tale of the psychological consequences of being an unwanted
child who is lost in a welter of lies about where he came from. It is
this unwanted child who is most vulnerable to murderous and
incestuous fantasies and action. So, if we take Oedipus's adoption
as central to his conflict, then Oedipus's actions were the result of
the deception that was inflicted upon him. It was Laius and Jocasta,
and later Polybus and Merope, who "turned a blind eye" to the
truth of their actions and, as a consequence, left Oedipus vulnerable to breaking the law on incest and parricide through ignorance.
In *Oedipus the King*, we are moved not because, as Freud believed,
our deepest desires are revealed to us, but because we are caught
up in a double vision. We know Oedipus's past, but he does not,
and we, the audience, are suspended, helpless but longing to avert
the tragedy that will overcome Oedipus. This agonizing place, into
which Sophocles puts the audience, derives much of its power from
our knowledge and from Oedipus's ignorance of his generational
history.

There is a body of psychoanalytic literature, beginning in the
late 1960s, that has been concerned with the effects of adoption on
infant psychic development. Most now agree that there is no special
pathology that is associated with adoption; nevertheless, there is a
common agreement that adopted children and their adoptive
parents do face considerable unconscious conflicts (Blum, 1983;
Brinich, 1995; Colarusso, 1987; Glenn, 1974; Nickman, 1985; Ross,
1982; Sherick, 1983). Typically, the parents will be facing their own

infertility, and this will have a powerful impact upon the adopted child's anxiety about his own sexuality and fertility. The adopted child, whether it has been told or not, seems to have an intuitive sense of being different. When the child knows of its adoption there will be anger with the abandoning parents and anxiety that the adoptive parents may abandon them. This is often followed by the adopted child pushing away the adopting parents, while being filled with beliefs about "being a messy dirty child, a slut, or a murderer (sometimes specifically a parricide)" (Brinich, 1995, p. 185). All these authors agree that fears and wishes about incest can become a preoccupation.

Allied with the adopted child's belief that he is dirty, a slut, and a murderer, there will be a distortion in what Freud called "the family romance" (1909c). The "family romance" that many children imagine is that they are adopted children and that their real parents are illustrious and famous people with whom they will eventually be reunited. Freud understood these romances as representing the ambivalent feelings that children face towards their parents as they grow up. For the adopted child, their "family romance" will necessarily be different. They have to face that they actually have "good parents" who adopted them and "bad parents" who abandoned them, and these images of the good and bad parent will fluctuate and upset the child's emotional balance, as the child faces developmental challenges and the need to find a way of accommodating ambivalent feelings. The abandoning parents may become the fantasized ideal parents, especially in adolescence, when the adoptive parents may be experienced as oppressive. It is significant that Oedipus was only sixteen or seventeen when he left his adoptive parents (Vellacott, 1971; Bowlby, 2007). In a footnote (p. 171, n. 5), Bowlby suggests that though there is no mention of Oedipus's age in the play, there may have been a "temporal symmetry" of sixteen years between Oedipus's first appearance at Thebes and marriage to Jocasta and the recurrence of the plague sixteen years later. In other words, Oedipus was sixteen when he married Jocasta.

One of the most powerful fantasies that confronts an adopted child, when he does not know about his family of origin, is the exciting fear of incest. When the adopted child knows that his parents are not his true parents, and his siblings are not birth siblings, the incest taboo can seem more porous or less firmly in place. The fantasy can go two ways. If the "true" parents are not known, then they may be unknowingly encountered, at a crossroad, and incest might follow. The other fantasy is that if one's parents are not one's "true" parents, then there may be an anxiety about what holds the incest taboo in place, both on the side of adopted parents and of their adopted children (Blum, 1983; Brinich, 1995; Glenn, 1974; Lord, 1991; Wieder, 1977).

This two-way fantasy about incest is what Oedipus faced as he fled from Corinth, suspecting that his parents, Polybus and Merope, were not his true parents. He fled from his adopted parents because he feared the incest taboo would not hold with them. That is to say, he was more vulnerable to incestuous and destructive desires. But he also faced the possibility that he would meet his "true" parents at the crossroads of his life and would not know who they were, and incest could follow.

The theme of murder, or parricide in the case of Oedipus, is a powerful anxiety that faces the adopted child. The wish to eliminate anyone who causes pain is a common infantile response to conflict. In a "good enough" family it is an acceptable emotion that is accommodated and in time becomes ameliorated. For the adopted child, the intensity of the emotion is heightened as he comes to terms with the knowledge that his identity has been compromised by his progenitors. His generational history has been eliminated, and he is left split between the wish to murder his murderers and the anxiety that he is the murderer. For example:

> George [a 7 year old adopted child] . . . told his therapist that he had a mother, but she had been shot and killed by his father. However . . . [George] had avenged his mother's death when he was 4 years old by killing his father himself. [Wagonfeld & Emde, 1982, p. 92]

or

> Ron's [a 12 year old adopted child] attempt to relate his emerging sexuality to his biological parents continued, as did his intense struggle with anger at the biological father . . . "If he is not dead, I'll kill him". [Colarusso, 1987, p. 228]

Oedipus enacted the two most strongly held fantasies that the adopted child has to face. He actually murdered the father who had behaved so murderously towards him, and he bound himself, destructively, to the woman who had colluded in his abandonment, but these tragedies were the consequence of his ignorance and the deceit that had been inflicted upon him.

Though *Oedipus Rex* was written over two thousand years ago, Sophocles' acute psychological perception that ancestral history plays a large part in personal identity still holds true. This truth seems to born out in the works of a modern playwright, Edward Albee, who, in many of his plays, elaborates the theme of adoption and violence and death. Some commentators have suggested that Albee's own adoption when he was eighteen days old has played a significant part in the adoption theme that runs through many of his plays (Blum, 1969; Glenn, 1974; Siegel & Siegel, 2001). In a recent interview entitled "Who am I?", in the *Guardian* in 2007, Albee said he had the fantasy that he must have "an identical twin brother somewhere . . ." and then added that all his writing had been about a search for his family and his identity. "I suspect that every play I write is part of one large play. But you don't know the large play till you've written the last one" (Rocamora, 2007). One reason that has been given for Albee's search for his missing family and identical twin has been linked to the difficulty he had in adjusting to his adopted family and their values (Kolin, 1988).

A play that continues Albee's theme of "Who am I?" is *The Goat, or Who is Sylvia*, which was produced at the Almeida Theatre in London in 2004. Albee wrote about this play, "Every civilization sets quite arbitrary limits to its tolerance . . . It is my hope that people will think afresh about whether or not all the values they hold are valid" (Albee, 2004). In other words, the audience was warned that the play was set to challenge the "limits of tolerance". Overtly, Albee asked us to imagine bestiality and to tolerate our thoughts about it. However, behind the image of bestiality lie much more poignant fantasies that have to do with adoption, incest, homosexuality, and sexual identity, and these fantasies link back to the problems that Oedipus faced. (I am much indebted to a conversation I had with Eilish Quinn about the role of adoption in this play.)

The explicit tragedy of this play centres upon a middle-aged man, Martin, who falls in love with a goat, and, as a consequence, his family life with his wife, Stevie, whom he loves faithfully and devotedly, and with his homosexual son, Billy, falls apart. It is a complicated play, and for some it remains opaque and unbelievable and for others it is thought to be a comedy. But if we keep in focus what Albee has told us, that all his plays are concerned with finding his lost family, then the play seems less opaque and much more tragic.

Albee gives the play two titles, *The Goat, or Who is Sylvia?* and these two titles signify the ambiguity of the imagery that surrounds the goat. *Who is Sylvia?* is the title of one of Schubert's most famous songs. The song itself comes from Shakespeare's, *Two Gentlemen of Verona*, a play that, via the device of cross-dressing (Julia dresses up as a man), questions the nature of true love (Shakespeare, 1966 [1623]). Albee then adds to the two titles in brackets (*Notes Toward a Definition of Tragedy*), and this seems to make a link to Greek tragedy. One characteristic of the plays of Aeschylus and Sophocles, considered above, is that there was a background story or myth that was familiar to the audience. It seems fair to assume that Albee's wish, to make known that all his plays are about a search for his family and the nature of true love, is the background myth that needs to be held in mind as we watch the unfolding tragedy of *The Goat*.

The play unravels with the discovery that Martin has fallen in love with a goat. Why a goat? Martin's son is called Billy, and so, putting Billy together with the goat raises the possibility that Albee is exploring complex issues to do with sexual identity between fathers and sons. *Who is Sylvia?*, the secondary title of the play, is the name he has given the goat, and this in turn suggests that the goat is also associated with the search for love of the mother. "Love doth to her eyes repair, / To help him of his blindness / And, being helped, inhabits there" (Shakespeare, 1966[1623]).

Martin is in the country looking for a retreat for himself and Stevie when he comes face to face with the goat looking through a gate. He has a moment of epiphany as he looks into her eyes.

> I knelt there, eye level, and there was a . . . an understanding so intense, so natural . . . And there was a connection there—a communication—that, well . . . an epiphany . . . and when that happens there's no retreating, no holding back. [Albee, 2004, pp. 51–52]

It is a compelling moment in the play, and evokes a sense that what Albee is describing is a moment of communication that goes beyond love. It is a moment of recognition. Yet, the goat is a denigrated and debased figure who blinds him and shatters every part of Martin's life as well. Oedipus' self-blinding is echoed in the image of Martin's encounter with the goat's eyes. Is she Jocasta? The shattering of Martin's life comes about through the impact that his love for the goat has upon his friend Ross, his wife Stevie, and his son Billy. The tragedy hinges upon the realization that the search for "true" recognition, the "connection", the "communication" when Martin looked into the goat's eyes, shatters the social structures that Martin had lived by. The adopted child can never have back what was taken away. Indeed, the moral of the play might be seen to suggest that the adopted child should not search for its true parents, for it is psychologically too destructive to "normal" family life.

Martin's collapse seems also to point back to the dilemma that Oedipus faced. How can you know who your parents are, if you have been abandoned? Where might you find them? When Martin fell in love with the goat, she stood as a symbol for that which can never be acceptable. Or, to put it another way, the goat stood for the tragic realization that you can never find your true parents, in the way the adopted child longs for. It is a fruitless and destructive search, for to trust the moments of epiphany can lead you into the by-roads of bestiality/incest/death.

There have been cases reported in the press, over the years, of siblings separated at birth who, on meeting in adult life, fall in love. The same is also true of parents who have given up their children for adoption. If they meet up when the child is grown up, they can both fall in love, and an incestuous relationship can take place, as I discovered in a group I ran for incest survivors. Such a phenomenon has been called "gender sexual attraction" (Gonyo, 1980). Gonyo wrote a book, *I'm His Mother, But He's Not My Son*, on her own personal experience of incestuous sexual desire for her son, whom she had given up for adoption at birth and re-met twenty-six years later. She suggested that the erotic arousal she felt may be the "missed bonding" that should have taken place at birth. The concept of "gender attraction" also seems to suggest a compelling unconscious force that links people who share the same genetic heritage. This may be a popular explanation for a sexual attraction that exists in all families. However, children who are removed from their family of origin are vulnerable to a longing to re-find and be reunited with those who abandoned them, and this compelling need can have tragic consequences if incest follows upon a reuniting, for, at the very least, such an action challenges society's ethical code against incest (Greenberg, 1993).

In this account, the finding of an unknown parent or sibling can be experienced as a moment of epiphany, as described by Albee when Martin falls in love with a goat. Albee's idea of Martin falling in love with a goat shocks us into recognizing a vulnerability in those who do not know where they come from. Vellacott had suggested that when Oedipus left Corinth, he might meet his parents anywhere in Greece, and it was this fact that made Oedipus vulnerable to the possibility that he might commit incest, unknowingly. Similarly, the goat could be seen as the symbol of the incestuous fantasy that accompanies the unknown and lost family.

There are other, darker fantasies of murder and homosexuality in Albee's drama, and these fantasies can be said to accompany the adopted child's search for sexual identity. The homosexual aspect of Albee's play links back to other myths of Oedipus that bring out his homosexual relationship with his father Laius and Chrysippus, the young son of the King of Pelops, whom Laius had seduced. For instance, Oedipus is seen as the *alter ego* of Chrysippus, that is to say, Oedipus avenges Laius's abduction of Chrysippus (Ross, 1982, p. 178). In another version, Oedipus falls in love with Chrysippus and fights Laius for him (*ibid.*, p. 64). It has already been mentioned that Martin's son is called Billy. The association to Billy and "billy goat" brings to our attention the complex image of the goat as an amalgamated figure of male and female. The adopted child needs a father as well as a mother, and, as in the Oedipus myth, the abandoning father seems to stir up violent fantasies around parricide. Stevie, Martin's wife, kills the goat and re-enters the stage, spattered with blood and carrying the body of the dead goat. This chilling action is reminiscent of bloodstained moments in Aeschlyus's *Oresteia*, when revenge stalked the stage with the murder of Agamemnon and Clytemnestra. In the case of Albee's play, Martin's murderous fantasies are enacted by his ambiguously named wife, Stevie. It is Stevie who expresses the rage against the goat, but it is not only her own rage against Martin for humiliating her; it also represents the murder of love, love between Stevie and Martin, and love between Martin and the goat. Finally, and perhaps most bleakly of all, it is Martin's response to the goat that unwittingly destroys his marriage and love for Stevie and his son Billy.

The homosexual theme, which has been present from the beginning in the character of Billy, comes to a painful climax. Martin and Billy are alone on the stage and Billy tries to explain how he is going to manage the knowledge that his father has fallen in love with a goat.

> Ya see, while great old Mom and great old Dad have been doing the great old parent thing, one of them has been underneath the house, down in the cellar, digging a pit so deep!, so wide!, so . . . HUGE! . . . we'all fall in and never . . . be . . . able . . . to . . . climb . . . out. . . again.

The stage instructions then read, "Billy wraps his arms around Martin . . . crying all the while. Then it turns—or does it?—and he kisses Martin on the mouth—a deep, sobbing, sexual kiss" (Albee, 2004, p. 64).

This deep, sobbing, sexual kiss represents the longing of a son for a father who has been lost. Martin has betrayed Billy and the effect upon the son of losing his father is that he falls into a black hole. Billy's solution, in order to climb out of that hole, seems to be that if he can sexually attract his father, then maybe his father will not leave him, but that would be an act of incest. If we now return to Albee's myth, that all his plays are searching for his "real parents", then he may be asking us to imagine that, like Oedipus, if we do not know who our fathers and mothers are, our lives are spent looking for them with a ferocity and passion. This ferocity and passion can lead unknowingly into tragedies that society cannot tolerate. Oedipus marries his mother and kills his father. Martin falls in love with a goat, Sylvia. Stevie murders the goat and the impact upon Billy is that he is left with an incestuous homosexual longing for his father. The destructive fantasies that can surround the adopted child, as he searches for his "true" parents are visited upon subsequent generations.

The opening question in this chapter concerned the effect upon psychic development if there was ignorance of ancestry. Sophocles'

Oedipus the King and Albee's *The Goat, or Who is Sylvia?* answer that question by showing that the child who is lied to about his past, or who is denied knowledge of his ancestry, is particularly vulnerable to the accident of incest, but also he is more prone to develop distorted fantasies of his true parentage that can act destructively upon his adult life. Oedipus enacts the two most powerful fantasies that accompany the unconscious life of the abandoned child: he murders his father and marries his mother. As recent commentators have suggested, he does not have the necessary resources to resolve his Oedipus complex (Bowlby, 2007; Faimberg, 2005). Albee, in a reworking of the Oedipus myth in his play, *The Goat*, elaborates the emotional distortion that accompanies the destiny of Oedipus, the adopted child.

CHAPTER THREE

Sibling ghosts

"An innumerable variety of cases can be thought of in which we should say that someone has pains in another person's body . . . or in any empty spot.

(Wittgenstein, 1933–1934, p. 50)

Aeschylus, Sophocles, and Albee seemed to share a common view that it is the hidden and unspoken traumas of loss, violence, and death that inscribe themselves upon the psyche of subsequent generations. In this chapter, the repercussions that a sibling death might have upon the whole family, including any surviving siblings, is explored. In particular, if the loss of a sibling is hidden or never adequately mourned and remembered, its voice can be heard in future generations. Psychoanalytic theory since Freud has neglected the possibility that their presence might be felt across several generations and might be demanding to be acknowledged. Loewald put this idea particularly well when he wrote,

Those who know ghosts tell us that they long to be released from their ghost life and laid to rest as ancestors. As ancestors they live forth in the present generations, while as ghosts they are compelled to haunt the present generation with their shadow life. [Loewald, 1980, p. 249]

To illustrate how this idea might be thought about is the following description from Dali about the effect of his dead brother, who preceded his birth.

> I experienced death before living life. . . . My brother died . . . three years before I was born. His death plunged my father and mother into the depths of despair. . . . And in my mother's belly, I already felt their anguish. My fetus swam in—a kind of theft of affection . . . This dead brother, whose ghost welcomed me . . . it is not by chance that I was named Salvador, like my father and like me . . . I learned to live by filling up the gap of affection which was not really given to me. [quoted in Schützenberger, 1998, p. 131]

It is particularly interesting that Dali felt he could experience his parents' anguish even in his mother's belly, for recent neurological research into the mother's state of mind during pregnancy seems to confirm such an idea (Gerhardt, 2005). Furthermore, the belief that he spent the rest of his life trying to find a way into his parents' heart is a profound insight into the effect that a dead sibling can have upon a surviving sibling.

Raphael-Leff has written on the traumatic effect the death of Freud's brother, Julius, had upon Freud's psychic development. She suggested that "the death of this baby (Julius) was probably the most significant emotional event in Freud's entire life and remained encapsulated as an unprocessed wordless area of prehistoric deathly rivalry and identification" (Raphael-Leff, 1990, p. 325).

This idea seemed to have been partially acknowledged by Freud when he wrote to Fliess on 3rd October 1897, "I greeted my one-year-younger brother . . . with adverse wishes and genuine childhood jealousy, and his death left the germ of [self] reproaches in me" (Masson, 1985, p. 268). We also learn in Raphael-Leff's detailed exploration of Freud's family history that his mother's brother, also named Julius, had died aged twenty, just one month before Freud's brother died.

Over the past thirty years, much research has been done on the mother's state of mind and its impact upon her children. In particular, the effect that a dead child can have upon the mother's mind and in her subsequent mothering capacities (Beebe & Lachmann, 2002; Emery, 2002; Fonagy, Steele, Moran, Steele, & Higgitt, 1991; Green, 1983; Jones, 2006; Stern, 1985; Winnicott, 1971, to name but a few). It is suggested that the mother might unconsciously expect that a surviving child should carry the image of the dead child, thus giving the surviving child two impossible tasks: to comfort the mother, and assuage her longing that the dead child might still live. With such an idea in mind, we could expect that the double grief of Freud's mother, Amalie, will have affected Freud, and will have given him an impossible task which he hints at in his self-reproaches about the death of his brother. We could imagine in Freud's "unprocessed wordless area of prehistoric deathly rivalry and identification", there will have been two rivals for Amalie's attention, his uncle as well as his brother. So, perhaps it is not only Freud's dead brother that "can be said to have 'possessed' psychoanalysis" (Mitchell, 2000, p. 232), but also his dead uncle haunts Freud's theories. In other words, psychoanalytic theory has not paid enough attention to intergenerational sibling loss, the loss of Freud's uncle Julius, as well as his brother Julius (Balint, 1993). Balint, writing on "Mr Smith", a "not-ordinary" patient who produced "not ordinary" feelings in the analyst, attributed his lack of memories of his early life to the fact that his mother had lost her brother when he was born and she had called him by his brother's name (*ibid.*, p. 86). She wrote that the mother had not been able to "accept him as a son" and, in so doing, "she denied him an existence" (*ibid.*, p. 106). "The effect of all this is to produce an intense desire and need to create [his] own words, images, sounds and movements, a need which may be a driving force in all artists" (*ibid.*, p. 108).

Green, in his paper "The Dead Mother" (1983), shows clearly the vital impact that the mother's state of mind has upon her children. The theme of his paper is the impact of maternal depression upon the mind of the infant. He suggests that if a mother becomes depressed during the early life of her child, she will necessarily withdraw from an active engagement with this child, who, in turn, will experience a catastrophic "hole". The reason for this catastrophe is that the mother will be experienced as "psychically dead in the eyes of the young child in her care". The psychic death of the mother will lead to the child being encapsulated in a tomb with the mother. The chilling result of this entombment with the mother, or, in Green's words, this "negative hallucination", is that the mother never psychically recovers for the child and never becomes a lively person with whom the child can identify. Instead, the child identifies with a "hole" where the mother had once been (*ibid.*, p. 142).

Some years after Green had written this paper, he was interviewed by Gregorio Kohon. In this conversation, he acknowledged that the concept of the "dead mother" stemmed from his personal experience of a depressed mother:

> I believe that the dead mother is a paper which has been valued not only because of its clinical finding, but because it is linked to a personal experience. When I was 2 years old, my mother had a depression: *she had a younger sister, who died after having been burned accidentally* . . . I can only suppose that I have been very strongly marked by this experience which, of course, needed three analyses to relive fully. [Kohon, 1999, pp. 13–14, my emphasis]

On this account, Green's mother became depressed following the death of her sibling.

But later on in this interview, Green reveals that his mother did not turn away from him when he was two and his aunt was burned to death. Green's mother was depressed already when he was born. At the time of his birth, his fourteen-year-old sister had just developed tuberculosis of the spine and had to be sent to hospital in France, where she remained for four years. He comments,

> My mother was—like any mother whose daughter was away because of an illness—very sad and depressed and my parents used to go for holidays to France as soon as the school stopped. They would spend two months there to enable my mother to stay with my sister. [*ibid.*, p. 11]

From this account, Green's mother was preoccupied at his birth and, therefore, we could surmise that, unlike those patients he describes in "The Dead Mother", he had not experienced a lively mother who became transformed overnight by "a change of fortune", but a mother already depressed and withdrawn.

Green's description of the "dead mother" is replete with words such as "entombment", "loss of meaning", "hole", "negative hallucination", "deathly deserted universe", "maternal necropolis". "A malediction weighs upon him" for "there is no end to the dead mother dying" (Green, 1983, p. 149). These chilling images seem to suggest that beyond the suffering of the child with its depressed and withdrawn mother, there lies Green's dead aunt encapsulated in his theory of the "dead mother". This dead aunt has echoes with the double encapsulation that Freud suffered with the death of his uncle and brother. The theories of both Freud and Green are haunted by dead and ill siblings across two generations, which give added weight to the doom filled concepts of the "death drive" (Freud, 1920g) and the "deathly deserted universe" (Green, 1983).

Where do we go from here, if, as Loewald suggested, we are to turn these ghosts into ancestors? What would it mean to bring Freud's uncle and Green's aunt into their theories? These questions led me to think about the case of a patient, Anna. What led her into her innumerable love affairs? She never achieved the happiness she believed was owing to her, and, consequently, when the latest affair ended, she would take an overdose. She hoped that this gesture would bring back her lost love. I failed to grasp the message that lay hidden in her behaviour and she left therapy abruptly in pursuit of a new love. It is only now that I can begin to imagine the "deathly deserted universe" that haunted her.

Anna was the younger of two children. She had an older brother. I knew her mother had lost her only sibling, a brother, when she was a child. I knew little about her father, except that Anna believed he preferred her to his wife. When Anna was seven or eight, her brother, who was several years older, developed polio that left him crippled for life. Her place as the youngest child and the supposedly adored daughter of her father was challenged by her brother's illness. Both mother and father, she felt, abandoned her in their concern for her brother. The deadly repetition that she continued throughout her adult life, and that I did not understand, was driven by her unconscious identification with her paralysed brother. She would offer herself up to her latest lover, full of excited expectation and then discover that, at the point of contact, her desire disappeared and she became frigid.

It seemed she had to remain in a paralysed place, for she was searching for the attention her brother had received from their parents. Her unconscious fantasy was that if she became a frigid invalid without desire, she would regain the narcissistic supplies that had been so abruptly withdrawn from her when her brother became ill. It was not surprising that she broke off therapy, for I repeatedly failed to understand her unconscious identification with her paralysed brother.

It is in reflecting on failed therapies or moments of impasse that I have been led to think about secret identifications. I have in mind those moments when the therapy seems lifeless and dead, or when we are in the grip of what Freud called "a negative therapeutic reaction" in which "the need for illness has got the upper hand in them over the desire for recovery" (Freud, 1923b, p. 49). I see now that the struggle might be, rephrasing Green, to make known the extreme ambivalence about bringing the dead or damaged sibling back to life.

For instance, to return briefly to Aeschylus, the moral legacy of the *Oresteia* seemed to be that no traumatic experience or deed can remain hidden without it having destructive consequences upon later generations. The traumatic deed not only needed to be acknowledged and spoken about, but the historical conditions in which the trauma was embedded had to be recognized. I failed to take account of the historical conditions of Anna's trauma when her brother became ill with polio, and I had forgotten that her mother had lost her sibling.

The idea that a trauma carries a history across the generations is readily acknowledged by many French analysts. They bring a wide-angled view about the world into which we are born; a world already structured by language and our parents' expectations (Abraham & Torok, 1994; Davoine & Gaudillière, 2004; Faimberg, 2005; Lacan, 1969–1970; Laplanche & Pontalis, 1964) and in which "an adult proffers to a child verbal, non-verbal and even behavioural signifiers which are pregnant with unconscious sexual significations" (Laplanche, 1989, p. 126). From this broader perspective, it makes sense to imagine that Oedipus was a victim of his parents' narcissism.

These analysts have explored beyond the impact of the world we are born into and addressed the question as to whether a present neurosis or psychosis has an historical link with trauma that may have occurred in a previous generation (Abraham & Torok, 1994; Davoine & Gaudillière, 2004). It seems they are acutely sensitive to the past two hundred and thirty years of war in France, from the French Revolution, the Franco–Prussian War, and the annexing of Alsace–Lorraine to the First World War and the divisive effects of the German occupation during the Second World War.

For instance, Davoine and Gaudillière (2004) draw upon their experience of being children of the Second World War. This leads them to extend an imaginative sympathy for those who have become mad as a result of family trauma such as war or sudden death. They believe that those who are driven mad are "the subjects of historical truth cut off from history". This idea is explored in detailed case histories and the analysis of literary and analytic figures in their book, *History & Trauma*. The subtitle of this book reads, *Whereof One Cannot Speak, Thereof One Cannot Stay Silent*. The subtitle is taken from Wittgenstein's first philosophical work, the *Tractatus*, in which the opening sentence reads, "The world is everything which is the case" and the closing sentence ends with "Whereof one cannot speak, thereof one must be silent". Wittgenstein was searching for the building blocks of logic as a way of distinguishing philosophy from the natural sciences or psychology. And when he wrote the *Tractatus* (1918) he believed that he had discovered what was known as the picture theory of language. Logical properties do not "say" anything. "Logical so-called properties *show* the logical properties of language and therefore of the universe, but *say* nothing" (Wittgenstein, 1914, p. 102). Davoine and Gaudillière do not have such philosophical concerns. In fact they turn Wittgenstein's injunction upon its head and suggest one must struggle to find a language "whereof one cannot speak". It is being silent that can send one mad, though the problem is to find the appropriate words and the necessary silence in the face of a petrifying disaster.

Davoine and Gaudillière take up the language of Lacan and suggest that a catastrophic event can breach the psychic world. For Lacan (1969–1970), there are three levels within the psyche. There is the Imaginary, the Symbolic, and the Real. The Real is the no-go area of the psyche. It must never be breached. However, when there is a trauma that overwhelms the psyche, the Real is invaded and a psychic catastrophe takes place:

> Here we once again find the terms that are the ones I defined as
> fixing the category of the Real, insofar as it is radically distinguished,

in what I am articulating, from the Symbolic and the Imaginary—the Real is the impossible. [*ibid.* p 143]

[if] . . . the impact of the Real is brought to bear upon the subject . . . he has entered the zone of chaos in which the feelings of being oneself are compromised. [*ibid.*, p.14]

The most graphic representation of this catastrophe, or, as Lacan put it, "the impact of the Real", that Davoine and Gaudillière return to on many occasions, is war, for it shatters the psychic representation of space and time and can send people out of their mind, as can be seen from Bion (1982), in which he wrote that he had died after witnessing the traumatic death of Sweeting near the end of the First World War. Bion noticed that Sweeting "looked horribly anxious, almost ill . . . I looked at his chest. His tunic was torn. No, it was not his tunic, the left side of his chest was missing". As Sweeting was dying, he turned to Bion and said, '"You will write to my mother? You *will* write sir, won't you?" . . . And then I think he died. Or perhaps it was only me" (*ibid.*, pp. 248–249). Sixteen pages later, Bion went back to that scene and wrote, "Oh yes, I died—on August 8th 1918" (*ibid.*, p. 275).

In Lacanian terms, Davoine and Gaudillière suggest that what makes it difficult to find the words to structure the experience is that there has been an "epistemological rupture" that freezes space and time (2004, p. 88). Nothing can any longer be guaranteed. This is similar to the place of "entombment", where there is a "loss of meaning", a "hole", a "deathly deserted universe" of "negative hallucination" that Green described.

To give an example of their work, Davoine describes the case of a young man, Ernest, who had been hospitalized during a delusional breakdown and was taken into analysis. He came to a session in the middle of summer with a yellow woollen scarf tied round his neck. Davoine was shocked and asked him why he was wearing the scarf, and he told her he was ". . . holding my head on my neck". When Davoine asked him, "Whatever for?", he replied, "Because I have a girl's head on a boy's body" (Davoine & Gaudillière, 2004, p. 88). He then revealed that when he was ten years old, he had been wearing the same scarf when he had discovered a photograph of a baby. He had asked his grandmother who the baby was, thinking that it was probably a photograph of himself. His grandmother told him that she was his sister, who had died before he was born. At the same time, she told him he had had a brother who had died after he was born from the same congenital deformation of the spine.

No one in the family had talked about his two dead siblings, though Davoine believed that he knew unconsciously of his dead sister through the way his mother had handled him. Davoine suggested to him that he had been driven out of his mind because he carried the unspoken grief and shame of his parents and grandparents at the loss of his two siblings. As Davoine helped him to speak about his dead siblings, his delusions disappeared and he gave up his own suicidal mission to join them. Ernest was an extreme case of psychosis, and it is not clear if there were other sibling deaths in previous generations that added to the shame that his parents and grandparents had felt. Nevertheless, the case of Ernest illustrates the fact that traumatic events such as death do not remain hidden, though the expression of the trauma may take a bizarre form.

To return to the question of how to turn ghosts into ancestors, it seems, from the account above of Davoine and Gaudillière, that one of the first points of entry into understanding individual suffering is to take an account of the family history across several generations. It is with that thought in mind that I end the chapter with a case history of a patient, Muriel, who displayed some of the characteristics that seem common to all those who suffer a trauma. She was cut off from her own desire. It was our search for a meaning to her present impasse that led us to discover a trauma that had stretched across three generations.

Muriel came to see me because, entering her forties, she had never managed to form a close relationship with a man. She also wished she had been able to have a child. It became clear as we worked together for several years that her unmarried state and her anxiety about men had some link with an uneasy relationship with her mother. As our work deepened and she could share more confidently the feelings she had about her mother, I began to have quite strong anxieties about Muriel that I thought might echo the feelings her mother had had about her daughter. For instance, I would find myself becoming unusually worried about Muriel's health when she complained that she had an ache or pain. On other occasions, I would wonder why I had taken on such an unco-operative and difficult patient. In other words, I became aware of quite extreme feeling states in myself, and this led me to wonder whether I was picking up some of the states of mind of Muriel's mother. Was there a generational transmission of anxiety about survival that was pressing for words?

I began to imagine Muriel's mother and how she might have felt when Muriel was born. Had Muriel been a wanted baby? I decided to ask Muriel what she knew about her own birth and her mother's childhood history, and this is what I learnt. Muriel's mother, whom I shall call Ruth, was born in 1913 just before the outbreak of the First World War. She had been the oldest child. There had followed, quite quickly after the war had begun in 1914, a sister who was sickly and needed a lot of maternal care. Ruth's father—Muriel's grandfather—did not return from that war. He was never referred to again in Ruth's family.

These facts helped me to think further about my own feelings of concern and dismay that could be aroused when I was working with Muriel. The points that I kept in mind were: Muriel's mother Ruth had an ill sister, Muriel's aunt. Ruth also had a grieving mother, Muriel's grandmother, added to which Ruth had lost her father, Muriel's grandfather. I speculated that Ruth's internal world contained an ill sister, a distressed mother, and an abandoning father. I then assumed Ruth would have brought these emotional experiences to her mothering of Muriel, and this was reflected in my anxious ambivalence towards Muriel.

It seems that Ruth grew up well enough and married a military man when in her mid-twenties, but tragedy hit her again. The Second World War broke out when Muriel was two. Muriel's father was captured early on in the war and just survived the ferocious experience of a concentration camp in the Far East. He returned when Muriel was seven, a damaged man physically and mentally, and he died soon after. Ruth did speak of him to Muriel, and his photograph was hung on a wall, but Muriel could not find any emotional attachment to him. He was a stranger or an unknown relative whose lifeless portrait she passed each day. Ruth did not help to bring him alive with any memories of him and, as a result, Muriel "forgot" to ask her mother about him. He seemed to Muriel to be as lifeless as her unmentioned grandfather.

How did all these losses impact upon Muriel, and what link might there be with her failure to marry and her longing for a child? We would go over these difficulties and together we would speculate about the possible impact that her sickly aunt or her dead grandfather had had upon Ruth's capacity to mother Muriel. We would also cruise around her father and his death, but he never seemed to come into a sharp emotional focus. It seemed clear that Muriel's uneasy relationship with her mother—such as I experienced in the countertransference—played an important part in her present stalemate with me. But we neither of us felt that our understanding of the past had liberated her into a more lively place within herself.

This period of stalemate coincided with the popular acclaim of Pat Barker's trilogy on the First World War, *Regeneration* (1993). Muriel became quite obsessed by these books, and I wondered if her obsession went beyond the literary merit of them. I asked her if there was someone else who had been left out, unnoticed, in Muriel's own family? Muriel's reply was to bring a photograph of a paternal uncle whom she had never known, but whose portrait she had constantly looked at because it had hung on the wall beside her father. He was her father's much older brother, who had been killed in the First World War.

What was significant about this discovery was that the uncle became the focus of Muriel's and my attention. He became the emblem of death that had stalked through two generations of Muriel's family. Muriel knew that this uncle had been a war hero and that her father had lived under his shadow. But why did this dead uncle help us to unlock unmentionable grief? When Muriel brought the photograph of her uncle, and we began to talk about the deaths that had cut through the foundations of her family, it was as though she was at last bringing a lost bit of herself that had become identified with all these dead men.

The uncle took up a central place in the therapy thereafter, for he helped Muriel to straddle the divided images of a distant father and a shadowy maternal grandfather. But there was more to him than an emblem, for, as we were to discover, Muriel had secretly identified with him and his unmarried state. He was her "safe" hero, and by "safe", I want to indicate that Muriel had invested him with a meaning that could remain secret from her mother. He lived eternally and unchanging in her mind until she began to tell me about him.

It may seem strange to postulate that Muriel's dead uncle could help us unravel some of the traumatic losses in Muriel's family of origin. How can an uncle, whom Muriel never knew, come to represent or gather up the dead figures that stalked her life? And why would she have identified with him? It might be said that Muriel's uncle was no more than a metaphorical representation of her dead father and grandfather. And I was inclined at first to believe that, until he began to have a life of his own in the therapy and the mood of the sessions began to change. I began to have a strong sense of his presence that puzzled me. Who was he for Muriel? Had she filled the "hole" or "gap" in her psyche, as a result of her father's premature death, with a secret alliance with her uncle? Did that idea provide a clue to the difficulty she had in imagining she could be a wife and mother? Were they secretly entombed together, uncle and niece? If we return to Dali's autobiographical writing, as quoted at the beginning of this chapter, it is clear that his sense of himself was forged upon the death of his brother. In other words, his self-identity was linked to his generational history, as he tellingly said, "I learned to live by filling up the gap of affection which was not really given to me". Had Muriel filled up the "gap of affection" that had been lost at her father's death with an image of her uncle?

When Muriel brought me the photograph of the dead uncle, we began to discuss him in relationship to Muriel's father, and there was, as I said, a palpable shift in the mood of the sessions. We became like siblings—she was an only child—engaged in a fascinating task of understanding the older generation. I felt myself becoming the sister she had longed for, and with whom she could share the secrets of her family, out of earshot of her mother. And this shift in the transference helped me to think about the parallel sibling relationship between Muriel's father and her uncle. Muriel felt she had lost out in never having a sibling, whereas her father had had a sibling whom he had lost. We began imagining her father and his brother together and reconstructing the meaning that these two brothers had for each other, and then something surprising happened. We could both begin to feel the impact of the uncle's death, and this led her to thinking about the impact of his death upon her grandparents.

Several sessions later, Muriel returned in a fury. She had nearly torn up the worn photograph of her dead uncle. She said she was fed up with all her family and not least this seemingly heroic uncle. He had trapped them all and she hated her grandparents for idealizing him. She almost shouted as she said, "No-one has been able to move from the hallowed ground he seemed to stand upon." In her mind, she wanted to wrench his portrait down from the wall beside her father. I was surprised at this turn of emotion, but it felt more engaged and alive, even though I was to blame, she said, for all this distress.

Over several weeks, we gradually discovered a deeply held fantasy that had kept her lifelong grief and anger at bay. Muriel had never had help to face her grief at her father's death because Ruth herself had not been able to mourn the death of her own father. Both women were locked into rigid fantasies about the power and fragility of men. However, I reminded Muriel that she had had an experience that had been denied her mother. Ruth's father had died when she was still an infant in arms. Muriel had actually known her father twice, first when she was two and again, for a grievously short time, when she was seven. I suggested to her that her uncle held the clue to the idea that her father was alive in her mind, for she could feel passionately about this dead uncle whom she had never known. The discrepancy in the way she talked of her uncle in our sessions while she was significantly empty of sympathy and emotion for her father led me to believe that she had wrapped herself up in a close and secret identification with her uncle, her father's brother, as a way of holding on to her father, in a timeless space.

I shared with her my feeling that her fury was to do with the fact that we had cracked open this timeless fantasy and now she was faced with the legacies of death and distress across two generations. No wonder she was fed up. She very painfully came to see that she had denied a meaning to her father's death. She also realized that she had not been helped by her mother (hence, another reason for her angry outburst), for her mother had had no language to help her. She could see that Ruth had been forced to deny the meaning of her own father's death a generation before and, as a result, had been unable to help Muriel. Mother and daughter shared a common graveyard, as it were, but had had no language to speak of their sadness.

Once Muriel could feel that she had blocked off any feeling about her father's death, we could begin to think about the "gap" or "hole" that had been left in her psyche by his abrupt departure, similar to that described in Green's paper, "The Dead Mother". Once she had neared the imaginative leap of feelings about her father, I asked her to imagine the sort of man her father might have been. I wondered aloud if she could imagine the effect that the death of her uncle might have had upon her father psychically. At the time, she was holding her uncle's photograph in her hand, and she became overwhelmed by emotion and started to cry. She was visibly shaken as she allowed herself to think about her father's grief at the death of his brother, and soon she began to imagine that she might also have suffered a similar emotion when her father died.

There was another emotional legacy that Muriel carried from her father. Her father had been burdened with the emotional knowledge that his brother was an idealized hero in his parents' mind. He could not replace his dead brother and become a hero to comfort them. Indeed, he died in a condition of defeat, for, mentally and physically, he had been destroyed as a consequence of his suffering in a concentration camp. Intuitively, Muriel would have picked up his depressed state of mind when he returned from war. I took up the idea that he died under the shadow of his heroic brother, for, at the time, I found myself imagining this uncle's portrait on the wall. As I began to imagine this portrait, I was filled with an all-consuming rage, similar to that which Muriel had brought a few sessions before. When I wondered further about this powerful emotion, I realized that what I had failed to understand was the father's ambivalence about his dead heroic brother. I shared with Muriel my sense that her father had held complex feelings about his brother, but she was shocked. In her fantasy about sibling relationships, they were always harmonious and nurturing, as she had felt with me. We explored further our "sibling" relationship, and she came to realize that it was an idealized fantasy. This fantasy about our "sibling" relationship helped her to wonder whether she had picked up a similar belief that her father had had about his brother. She slowly began to understand that her father might have had more ambivalent feelings about his brother, and this, in turn, led her to think more about why she had been shocked by my comment. She could begin to feel how the shadow of her idealized uncle might have oppressed her father and made him feel depressed and hopeless. If, indeed, she had intuitively picked up her father's despair, she could see that she might have felt the need to protect her dying father from his sense of failure at not being able to replace his brother in his parents' mind. She became visibly distressed in a session in which she imagined that the only comfort for her father was for her to become his "heroic" brother. Kestenberg had written about a patient, Rachel, who had identified with her dead grandmother as a way of comforting her father, and, in the same way, Muriel held within her a secret identity with her dead uncle, as though in this way she could bring her uncle back for her father (Kestenberg, 1980).

When Muriel ended the therapy, we both agreed that her unconscious identification with her dead uncle had imprisoned her. It had been a "heroic" act on her part, born out of her fervent wish to comfort her father. Understanding something of the complexity of this unconscious fantasy, she came to see that she had been held in a deathly embrace of unacknowledged grief and rage, occasioned by two World Wars, that had stretched back at least three generations on both sides of her family. We were both grateful to the photograph of her uncle, for he had helped us to think about the place he held in her family and, in turn, this allowed Muriel to begin to feel the sadness of her father's early death. Her feelings about her mother shifted once she could imagine her mother's unacknowledged grief for her father, Muriel's maternal grandfather. Finally, she felt less angry with her paternal grandparents for their idealization of their "heroic" son. Her family no longer needed rescuing from their suffering and she could begin to imagine a life of her own.

In this exploration of the manner in which trauma can be transmitted across the generations, it is notable that a dead sibling, such as Muriel's uncle, can hold a clue to much conflict and pain. It is true that, unlike Freud or Green, Muriel was not traumatized herself by a dead sibling; nevertheless, the significance of her dead uncle upon her father and her grandparents warranted my using her case material to illustrate the way a dead sibling can take possession of a family. We might identify, in partial ways, with many more members of our extended family than our mother or father. As long as Muriel's identification with her dead uncle remained secret, she was imprisoned and had to block her desire for a husband and child.

CHAPTER FOUR

Grandmother's footsteps

I n the Preface, I recounted a dream that a patient had brought me, in his penultimate session, about going to his grandmother's house for a meal. I had failed to recognize that he might have been telling me that his nurturing grandmother had been remembered and restored through our work together. At the time, I had never thought that there might be a significant grandparent within the internal world of the developing grandchild that might lie unrecognized. I had certainly not given much thought to the unconscious influence of my grandparents on my emotional development.

When Freud's father died in 1896, Freud has told us that it left him in a state of confusion and guilt, as he struggled to give meaning to the influence that his father had upon his psychic life. What impact did his father's death have upon Freud's fathering of his own children, and how did his children react to the loss of their grandfather and to Freud's grief (Masson, 1985)?

We know Freud reacted with anxiety to the death of his own grandfather from an anxiety dream he recounts in *The Interpretation of Dreams*, which he thinks he had when he was about seven or eight years old. He dreams of "My beloved mother, with a peculiarly, peaceful, sleeping expression on her features, being carried into the room by two (or three) people with bird's beaks and laid upon the bed". In one of his associations to the dream he says, "The expression on my mother's features in the dream was copied from the view I had had of my grandfather a few days before his death as he lay snoring in a coma" (Freud, 1900a, p. 583).

That dream is not the end of Freud's thoughts about his grandfather, for one year later he wrote,

> One of my brother's admonitions lingered long in my memory. "One thing", he said to me, "that you must not forget is that as far as the conduct of your life is concerned you really belong not to the second but to the third generation in relation to your father." [Freud, 1901b, p. 220]

There have been many interpretations others have made of Freud's dream, but Freud's two comments about his grandfather are a reminder that the way life and death are recognized within family history can be full of conundrums (Anzieu, 1986; Green, 1983). The death of a grandparent might give rise to questions about our relationship to them. There might be fantasies that they were our real parents. Maybe, like Freud, making sense of the anxiety that is aroused by the death of a grandparent might make one imagine "how different things would have been if I had been born the son not of my father but of my brother" (Freud, 1901b, p. 219–220). The generational confusion that can follow the death of a grandparent is not unique to Freud, though he had more reason than most to wonder about his generational history. Freud's father, Jacob, was already a grandfather when Freud was born. Jacob had been married twice before he married Amalie, Freud's mother, and he had two grown-up sons, Emanuel and Philipp. Emanuel was twenty-three and was married with a son, John, who was one year old when Freud was born. Freud, at birth, was an uncle to his nephew John. Philipp, Freud's other half-brother, was twenty and the same age as Freud's mother, Amalie. Indeed, there is evidence that Philipp took over the running of the Freud household when Jacob was away on his frequent business trips. As well, it was Philipp who famously accused Freud's nanny of stealing Freud's toys and money, and had her imprisoned, when Amelie was giving

birth to Freud's sister, Anna. To add to Freud's confusing generational history, he also suffered the trauma of his younger brother,
Julius, dying when Freud was seventeen months old. Amalie not
only lost her second son, but had just lost her brother Julius, whom
her son had been named after. When Freud was nine or ten (not
seven or eight, as he remembered in his dream), his maternal
grandfather died. Losses, generational confusion, and maternal
depression are part of the landscape of psychoanalysis, as well as
part of Freud's psychological heritage.

More importantly, what Freud's musings about his grandfather
reveal is that he holds a significant place within Freud's unconscious fantasies. Yet, in spite of Freud's thoughts about his grandfather, he did not pursue him into the internal world or consider the
place grandparents have in the structure of the psyche. One consequence seems to have been that there has been little clinical interest
in exploring the conscious and unconscious feelings that grandparents arouse. In 2011, on the PEP web of the Institute of Psychoanalysis, there were 1000 references to grandparents, mostly factual,
such as, "J went to stay with his grandparents when he was two".

One notable exception is Rosenfeld, who holds a passionate
belief that grandparents need to be given a voice in clinical work.
He believes that they provide "models" that have an independent,
nurturing, historical, and cultural place in the psyche, as he fondly
says about his own grandparents, and they keep alive "the music
of . . . childhood" (Rosenfeld, 2006). He wrote,

> Perhaps I have not learned from theories more than from my grand-
> mother in order to construct a model and be able to listen to, under-
> stand, and think about a human being who is talking of his life and
> his feelings. *I think my personal history determines the way in which
> I make use of my internal theoretical map.* [ibid., p.161, my italics]

His representation of his grandfather he experienced not so much
as a model, but more as someone who accompanied him in his day-
to-day analytical work. About one particular case he wrote,

> In the countertransference I felt moved and remembered vividly an
> important scene from my childhood with my own dear grand-
> father. I was able to deduce that L. had felt moved when he talked
> about his grandfather whom he loved so dearly, and he had found

in his treatment a place where he felt good, a simple place with good and abundant food. [*ibid.*, p. 135]

Others, who have also experienced the importance of grandparents within the internal world, seem to be suggesting that the unfolding of a present conflict can sometimes be understood within the embedded history of the grandparents (Balint, 1993; Faimburg, 2005; Kestenberg, 1972; Kestenberg & Kestenberg, 1982). The idea of the embedded history of the grandparents well describes those cases where the grandparents were not obviously apparent but had to be discovered, as though they were a secret, or, to use Rosenfeld's concept, they were held in "an autistic encapsulation" (Rosenfeld, 2006). In his Foreword to Rosenfeld's book, Ogden wrote, "This conceptualization of the function of autistic encapsulation as a sanctuary in which the healthy early experiences can be safeguarded from psychotic fragmentation is original to Rosenfeld" (Ogden, 2006, p. xiii). In all the clinical cases that these authors consider there was a traumatic history that centred around hidden and, in some cases, unknown grandparents. For instance, there was a case of a young anorexic girl whose self-starvation was a self-identification with a grandmother who had died in a concentration camp in the Second World War (Kestenberg & Kestenberg, 1982). In another case, the absence of a psychic life in a young man was attributed to the absent grandfather whose death during the Holocaust could not be acknowledged by the young man's father (Faimberg, 2005). Many of Rosenfeld's cases are second-generation survivors of the Chilean civil war, or the repressive regime of the military dictatorship in Argentina. They have lost parents and grandparents and, as a consequence, have lost their mind. In one case, Rosenfeld helps a young man out of his psychotic state of mind by recalling the songs his grandfather had sung him, and then they sing the songs together (Rosenfeld, 2006).

It is notable that Balint's work is slightly different in tone and feeling to the other psychoanalysts, who were working in the USA or South America. She was working in London, and she was not dealing with the traumatic experience of a grandparent prematurely torn away from the family by the Holocaust or civil war (Balint, 1993). The silent suffering of her patient, Kay, was entangled within the taboos and constraints of English culture. Kay's grandmother had an illegitimate child, Kay's mother, and this child was put into an orphanage and apparently forgotten about. The silent trauma that Kay carried unconsciously, which Balint called "a foreign body" was of Kay's mother's abandonment and Kay's grandmother's "unhealed wounds". This silent trauma was given voice by Kay's inability to leave her infant son, and was compulsively enacted by her need to restore antique furniture.

What is common to all these clinicians, who, it must be remembered, are concerned with the traumatic loss of a grandparent, is that they discovered an alive grandparent in the internal world of their patients. This alive grandparent was variously described as being represented in a "double identity" with the grandchild, or, more malignantly, as a "foreign body", or as being preserved in an "autistic encapsulation". These varying descriptions pick up a secret fantasy or alliance that these grandchildren create around their unknown grandparent. These grandchildren have all experienced unconsciously the distress and unhappiness of their parents' grief at the loss of the grandparent, even though the grandparent might never have been spoken of or referred to. They know their parents are grieving inconsolably. However, they unconsciously set about trying to console their parents through the means of this "double identity". They imagine that by becoming the grandparent, they can not only bring the grandparent to life, but at the same time they can restore their parents to their former wellbeing. The negative aspect of this heroic wish to comfort their parents is that these grandchildren become imprisoned. One young girl was starving herself to death (Kestenberg, 1980), a young man had absented himself from his life (Faimberg, 2005), another had gone mad (Rosenfeld, 2006), and Kay was trapped into compulsive behaviour (Balint, 1993).

In bringing out the similarities in the work of these authors, there is a danger that some of the more individual and unique aspects of their work are ignored. For instance, Kestenberg was working with Holocaust survivors and their children, and, in many cases, the children had been named after the dead grandparent (Kestenberg, 1980). So it was less surprising to discover that these children omnipotently believed they could bring back their dead grandparent and comfort their grieving parent. In the same vein, another analyst, working with the children of Holocaust survivors, went so far as to suggest that the suicide attempt of a young man had been impelled by the psychotic delusion that he could restore the grandfather/himself to his still grieving father (Kogan, 1992). But, whatever the traumatic conditions that led to the loss of grandparents, it seems that in all the cases considered the grandchildren will willingly, though unconsciously, take on any role that might rescue their parents from suffering.

It seems clear, thanks to the work of such clinicians, that the grandparents' footsteps can indeed be heard, whether they are unknown or have been unconsciously repudiated. In many cases, the grandparents are in secret hiding places and need to brought out if their grandchildren are to be free from carrying the pain of their death or disappearance. I end the chapter with a piece of clinical work on the effect that an unknown dead grandfather had upon the mind of his grandson, Nicholas, bearing in mind some of the thoughts of these writers. I want to emphasize that, in all my clinical cases in this book, I have picked out a piece of work that has seemed important, but it needs to be remembered that the particular work I highlight was, in all cases, within a more extensive context.

Nicholas had a paternal grandfather who had died before he was born. Nicholas came to see me when he was in his mid-twenties, following a breakdown that had required hospitalization. The early days of the therapy were spent trying to put together the pieces that had led to Nicholas's breakdown. He was very cut off, while at the same time obsessively anxious to tell the "truth". For instance, we spent many hours trying to make sense of his panic if he was late for a session or had forgotten to pay the bill. He believed if he "emptied" his mind of all his thoughts he would be safe. What I found puzzling was that his panic was followed by a compulsive need to promise me that it would never happen again. If I approached the question as to why I was such a persecuting figure who needed to be constantly reassured, he would seem to vanish in the session and his mind would go blank.

During one session, I found myself in an inward agony as he was giving me, yet again, a supposedly soothing explanation for a missed session. What was this about? Was he unconsciously projecting an infantile bit of himself? Alternatively, was I a heartbroken father or mother whom he was hoping to comfort? These questions filled my mind, and led me back to the work on generational trauma, quoted above. I recalled my experience with Martha (Chapter One) and Muriel (Chapter Three) and I felt more confident that I was picking up some as yet unknowable and unspoken secret. I asked Nicholas to tell me anything he knew about his family history. He was slightly annoyed at, and dismissive of, my question, saying he never spoke about his past because "he didn't believe in it". This amazing turn of phrase heightened my sense that perhaps I was in touch with a pain that Nicholas was carrying, but which he believed had no meaning. I was already becoming convinced he was carrying a double pain, his own and that of another.

I knew that Nicholas had been hospitalized because he had become uncontrollably violent at work; I also knew that when he presented himself at our first session he had specified the need for a "brief bit of counselling" because of what his mother called his "difficult temperament". I sensed that his difficulties, whatever they were, were embedded in a family system in which problems could be easily got rid of, or dismissed. Furthermore, there seemed an implicit belief that a violent action had no meaning, but was simply the expression of a "difficult temperament".

Nicholas had told me he was ashamed of his uncontrollable fits of rage. He would smash household items or hurl them around the room if he felt frustrated. He could be unreasonably angry at his work if the office was too noisy. A recent incident that had tipped him into fury had been when his boss had promoted him into a new office, where he would be on his own. It did not occur to him that there might be an explanation for these outbursts of rage, for he believed that he need only alter his "difficult temperament" in some way and his rage would be gone.

Gradually, Nicholas became more confident that his rage had a meaning rather than an unfortunate fact of his temperament. He began to have fleeting memories of his father in a fury. One incident in particular was vividly imprinted in his mind. The family was going out somewhere, but he and his sister were not ready on time. His father flew into an incandescent rage, and his rage was fuelled further when Nicholas's mother tried to calm him down. That was all Nicholas remembered of his father's anger. One might say he remembered someone out of control who could not be soothed, and here, surely, Nicholas was telling me of an identification with his father.

I began to ask Nicholas if he could imagine what his father's anger might have been about. Nicholas told me he knew nothing about his father, except his mother had told him that his paternal grandfather had died when his father was born. And then he said to me, in a sort of casual but slightly triumphant way, "Oh! by the way, did I ever tell you that my father left us when I was about six, and I have never seen him since!" I felt as if I had been hit in the stomach when Nicholas told me that he did not know his father. There had been nothing in the hospital notes that I had been given about a father who had abandoned the family, and I had, therefore, assumed he was still around. When I had recovered from my initial shock, I felt furious with Nicholas, as though he had deliberately deceived me. Then a sort of cold anxiety filled me as I began to believe he was more cut off and dissociated than I had imagined. Should I end the therapy? I certainly wanted to throw him out and wash my hands of this exhausting attempt to make sense of his violence. Finally, I felt he was ridiculing the whole enterprise of therapy, for he must have known that an event like his father's abandonment had some meaning. I could not respond in any way. I was silenced. But my silence was a deafening blow to Nicholas, who heard it as another abandonment and, as a consequence, he wondered whether he would ever be able to trust me again. Throughout the rest of therapy, we came back again and again to this moment. It was the reworking of this incident that led us to understand more about the link between Nicholas's violence, his father's abandonment, and his grandfather's death.

With my encouragement, Nicholas began to ask his mother about his father. We learnt that Nicholas's grandfather had been killed in a traffic accident when Nicholas's father had been born. Nicholas's father was an only child. His mother married again, but there were no children of the second marriage. Nicholas's father called his stepfather "Daddy" and he only discovered this "Daddy" was not his real father when he was grown up. He was furious, and walked out on his mother and stepfather, never to see them or speak to them again. He emigrated to South Africa. He met Nicholas's mother in South Africa and they married there, for that was where her family lived. Nicholas's father, it seemed, was a handsome and charismatic man, but he had a terrifying rage. Nicholas's mother became intimidated by him when they began to have children and the ordered and quiet house he needed was under threat with crying babies. She told Nicholas, regretfully, that she had gone along with the idea that when Nicholas was born he must be disciplined. He was not to be fed on demand, and if he cried, he must be put out of earshot. A strict military style regime was implemented from the moment of Nicholas's birth.

Family life became increasingly difficult to control when Nicholas's sister was born, and after a row, rather similar to the one Nicholas had already told me about, Nicholas's father walked out of the family. He severed all contact with his family, sent them no money, and the last that Nicholas's mother had heard about him was that he had contracted AIDS. It seemed that when Nicholas's father broke all relationships with his created family he was repeating the earlier walking out on his family of origin. But we did not understand the meaning of Nicholas's father's abandonment yet. Nicholas and his mother and sister left South Africa and came to live in England.

If the mother's account contained some of the historical facts about Nicholas's father, how did we make sense of Nicholas's violent behaviour? The first assumption I made was that Nicholas's father must have been traumatized by his father's death at his birth. As in the case of Freud and Green that I have discussed in Chapter Three, Nicholas's grandmother must have been depressed and grief struck, and perhaps she had been internalized as a "dead mother" by Nicholas's father. Adding to this trauma, we had to take on board that Nicholas's father had been deceived and betrayed by his mother when she did not tell him the truth about his stepfather.

We made several connections between Nicholas's violence and his father's traumatic history through the different ways we came to understand the effect that my "deafening silence" had had upon Nicholas, when I first learnt that his father had abandoned the family when Nicholas was six. It became clear that one aspect of my "deafening silence" echoed with Nicholas's infantile cries when he was put out of earshot. But this did not take us far enough in understanding Nicholas's outbursts of rage and my complicated emotional response when I learnt of Nicholas's father's abandonment. Once I knew that Nicholas's grandmother had lied to Nicholas's father about his stepfather, I could begin to process another aspect of my own wish to get rid of Nicholas. I felt I had been "deceived", but who was deceiving whom? Nicholas had already told me he did not believe in the past, and here he was unconsciously enacting that belief in casually telling me he had not seen his father since he was six. But now, something more complicated was happening. Another figure had entered. I felt that Nicholas and I were caught up in his grandmother's belief that her husband's death—Nicholas's grandfather—had no meaning or importance for her son. Here was an important deception that needed to be thought about.

I began to think about Balint's concept of a "foreign body" and Kestenberg's "transmitted traumatic neurosis". I was fairly confident that Nicholas's father had been doubly traumatized, first by the death of his father and the undoubted depression of his mother, but then by the lie under which he had been brought up about his true paternity, that is to say, the belief his stepfather was his real father. This led me to wonder whether part of Nicholas's rage was due to carrying the unconscious traumatic neurosis of his father. I approached this idea by asking Nicholas if he had any views about why his father had needed to organize his family as a military regime. Nicholas became extremely anxious, yet again, as he got in touch with his fear about being late for a session, and this led to a fantasy that all lateness represented potential chaos and abandonment. Nicholas retreated to a place of cold terror. It is hard to find the right words to express the emotions that seemed to shake Nicholas's body as he began to feel he was alone in his pram, out of earshot for a second time. For several sessions, he seemed in danger of acting so violently in the sessions that the therapy might break down irreparably. When he began to calm down, he told me that what seemed unbearable to him was that his agonizing experience of wordless terror was being added to by thinking about his father's state of mind. Nicholas had become temporarily convinced that I was intent upon sending him out of his mind.

During this difficult time, two clear images came to me. I could imagine Nicholas in his pram crying inconsolably until all hope had vanished, but now a more intrusive image came to my mind. I imagined his father "peering" into Nicholas's pram. I used the word "peering", for I was trying to get hold of the idea that something alien was being forced into Nicholas' psyche, as Nicholas had believed had been the case when I asked him to think about his father's state of mind. I recalled my strong feeling of wanting to get rid of Nicholas, but supposing I was wanting to get rid of Nicholas's father "peering" into Nicholas? It became possible to imagine that I was responding to the "foreign body" of his father's tormented mind that was being projected into Nicholas. I had consciously thought I wanted to push out Nicholas, for his violent behaviour was too much for me. But when I began to reflect upon his father "peering" into my mind, I came to see that what I wanted was to eject Nicholas's father from Nicholas's psyche. In other words, when Nicholas had first told me that he had had no contact with his father since he was six, there was an unconscious communication that I took time to process. Nicholas was trying to find a way of telling me that within his psyche there was the "foreign body" of his father's traumatic neurosis, but the only way he knew how to communicate this was by *not* telling me about his father and by not believing in the past, but this involved deceiving himself and me, as his grandmother had done.

The unconscious legacy of Nicholas's father's state of mind, precipitated by the death of Nicholas's grandfather and the deception of Nicholas's grandmother, took a long time to process. We entered a chilling world where there was a lack of tenderness and love and where cries were never heard. This experience had been repeated between Nicholas and myself when I first heard of his father's abandonment and had remained cold and silent. It was only through the slow process of understanding what had occurred between us that we could begin to make sense of an ancestral history in which Nicholas's father put his son out of earshot and then out of his mind, as he repeated what he felt had been done to him when his father, Nicholas's grandfather, died and his mother, Nicholas's grandmother, became a "dead mother" and deceived him.

All the way through this period of therapy, I found it hard to imagine how any man, when faced with his own vulnerable and dependent son, could turn away from an engagement of love and prefer to live cut off from human joy and pain. The cruelty and pain seem to stretch timelessly and I had to keep reminding myself that what had brought Nicholas into therapy was his own disengagement from himself and others. I would be failing Nicholas if I engaged in raging against his father's cruelty. Nicholas needed help to understand that he was repeating his father's response to conflict or pain by raging and breaking things up. Nicholas' identification with this neglecting father had to be faced in our work (Glasser, 1998).

Once we became within reaching distance of the idea that Nicholas was carrying within him a father who could not manage, Nicholas could begin to imagine that he need no longer worry about the effect he had had upon his father and, in the present, upon me, or anyone else. His father's immense suffering moved us both to tears once Nicholas had got beyond rage and identification with his father's cruelty. He realized how burdened he had been with anxiety to please his father and make him happy and bring him back. This allowed us to make sense of his need to tell the "truth" by "emptying" his mind. Nicholas had wanted to comfort his father by mothering him with truth rather than lies and deceit. Most importantly, Nicholas accepted the historical fact that his grandfather had died and his grandmother's deception had had a damaging effect upon his father's state of mind. It became possible for us both to imagine that the reign of cruelty that had unwittingly followed in the wake of his grandfather's death and his grandmother's deception no longer needed to be repeated in Nicholas's relationship to himself or in his encounters with other people.

In conclusion, it seems clear that grandparents create a structure within the internal world. They may be a role model or an ideal; the grandmother may need to be healed, as in the unconscious fantasy of Kay. There may be a hope that the grandparents can be secretly revived to comfort their suffering child. In the case of Nicholas, we discovered an unconscious fantasy that fathers and grandfathers and therapists "walk out" and leave a "deafening silence" that is unbearable until the fantasy of their cruelty can be brought to conscious memory and given some meaning.

CHAPTER FIVE

The nurse

"If the woman disappeared so suddenly, I said to myself, some impression of the event must have been left inside me. Where was it now?"

(Masson, 1985, p. 222)

In the previous four chapters, there have been some shadowy figures whose representation can be found in our inner world. These figures, such as grandparents, dead siblings, or abandoning parents can haunt later generations if they have been left in unmourned and unmarked graves. In my clinical work, a fuller and more detailed investigation into earlier family relationships has seemed to unburden the psyche of some who have been holding an unacknowledged family trauma. But, in filling in some of their fractured narratives, there is one "uninvited guest" who has been neglected: the wet nurse, the nurse, or nanny. She has been present in the history of child-rearing for the last 3000 years (Fildes, 1988), yet she is a scarcely mentioned figure in most accounts of psychological development. In this chapter, the emotional effect that wet nurses, nurses and nannies have upon children is explored and a question is raised about their absence from psychoanalytic theory and practice. Though the nurse or nanny is a figure who occurs within the family of the privileged, the wet nurse is a more ubiquitous figure upon whose breast the rich, the orphaned, and the poor have relied, and it is her legacy that can be heard in the voice of the nurse.

There are many literary and historical sources that acknowledge the significance of the nurse upon the child she looks after. Odysseus, on his return home to Ithaca, had his feet washed by his wet nurse, Eurycleia: "Of course, you are Odysseus, my dear child. And to think that I didn't know you till I'd handled all my master's limbs". At this moment Penelope, Odysseus's wife, has not recognized him. And, as Odysseus wants to remain unrecognized until he has made sure that Penelope has stayed faithful to him, he says to Eurycleia, "Nurse . . . do you wish to ruin me, you who reared me at your breast?" (Homer, 1946, p. 300). Two thousand years later, Churchill erected a memorial to his nanny, "Erected in Memory of Elizabeth Anne Everest who died 3rd July 1895 by Winston Spencer Churchill and John Spencer Churchill" (Churchill, 1930). And, in 1924, when her *Kinderfrau* died, Anna Freud is reputed to have said "[My *Kinderfrau* was] the oldest and most real relationship of my childhood" (Young-Bruehl, 1989, p. 398).

Though there are many literary testimonies to the love and devotion that the relationship between the nurse and the child can inspire, there can be conflicts that arise from the nature of the relationship itself. In Shakespeare's *Romeo and Juliet*, we witness the conflict of divided loyalties between a daughter, a mother, and a nurse, and we can begin to imagine that Juliet is also struggling between the psychic conflict of having "two mothers", one of whom is her nurse. (The estrangement from the mother when there have been a series of nannies who have been the principal caretaker is well summarized by one of my uncles, who said, "I have four aunts, one of whom is my mother.".)

From the very beginning of the play, Juliet is portrayed as more strongly attached to her wet nurse, who had breast-fed her for three years, than she is to her mother. When Juliet falls in love with Romeo, even though her parents want her to marry County Paris, she turns to her nurse to help her find a way to consummate her love for Romeo. However, when Juliet's father threatens to turn Juliet out of the house if she will not marry County Paris, the nurse sides with the parents and advises her to marry Paris, even though she knows where Juliet's true loyalties lie.

The significance of the nurse's change of mind hinges upon a conflict that all nurses face between the parents who employ them and the children they have nurtured. The nurse's role as a servant, who is dependent upon her employers, is in conflict with the relationship of love and trust she may have built up with the child she looks after. We see that the nurse and Juliet are caught up in an unfolding social tragedy that is exacerbated by the inequality created by the child-rearing practices of the day, in which babies were reared by wet nurses (Boswell, 1988; Gathorne-Hardy, 1993). It is not only the privileged middle classes who have employed wet nurses. Thomas Coram, when he set up his orphanage for abandoned children in London in the eighteenth century, would "farm out" these unwanted children to wet nurses in the country, sometimes for up to five years (Fildes, 1988). Juliet was not exactly farmed out, though she was left on her own with her nurse and the nurse's husband for long stretches of time while her parents were in Mantua.

We might suspect that Juliet's father, through the total lack of empathy he shows for his daughter, had also suffered a rupture from his own family of childhood. He raves at his daughter when she refuses to marry County Paris. He behaves like an infant in a temper tantrum when he is opposed. "Hang thee younge baggage, disobedient wretch / I tell thee what, get thee to the church a' Thursday. / Or never after look me in the face. / Speak not, reply not, do not answer me" (Shakespeare, 1994, Act III, Scene V). It seems of little concern to him what Juliet's feelings in the matter might be. It is for this reason I am imagining that Shakespeare understood that the child-rearing practices of wet nurses, which included "farming out", distanced privileged parents from their children and damaged those feelings of empathy and tenderness that parents might be expected to have for their offspring. Neither Juliet's mother nor her father treat Juliet as a person with her own feelings and desires; she is their commodity to be sold to the richest man available on the marriage market.

Juliet's parents are not part of her day-to-day upbringing; instead the nurse gives her the necessary warmth and love that all children need if they are to thrive. But Shakespeare also asks us to remember that the nurse's role in Juliet's life was at a high cost to herself. Her daughter, Susan, who was the same age as Juliet, had died from lack of milk. I do not know whether it is with a note of irony that Shakespeare has the nurse comfort herself with the words, "She was too good for me" (*ibid.*, Act I, Scene III), but Shakespeare lets us see into the complicated heart of a child-rearing practice that alienated children from their parents and instated a nurse as the surrogate mother. The nurse is the emotionally significant person in Juliet's life, and, at the same time, she is socially and economically powerless. Her ambiguous position is reflected when she realizes that she has to capitulate to Juliet's parents in spite of her love for Juliet. Juliet turns to her in despair when her parents are about to banish her for refusing to marry County Paris. "Oh! God Nurse, how shall these be prevented? / . . . What say'st thou, has thou no word of joy? / Some comfort nurse". And the Nurse replies, "I thinkest best thou marry with the County" (*ibid.*, Act III, Scene V).

The role of the nurse, in the unfolding tragedy in the lives of both Romeo and Juliet, hinges upon the ambiguity that is inherent in her position. The nurse and Juliet have a love for each other that is as strong as the love of a mother for her daughter, and yet neither was able to draw on that love to further the natural growth towards Juliet's maturing sexuality. Both of them were trapped in a pattern of child-rearing that created a conflict that they were powerless to counteract. Juliet's real mother and father had the social and financial power, the nurse had the emotional power, but this counted for nothing in the marketplace.

Another way of describing the tragic battle in *Romeo and Juliet* is to see it as a conflict between an emotional truth and an irrational system of child-rearing. This irrational system of child-rearing had culturally sustained the idea that the children should be "farmed out" and brought up by others (Boswell, 1988; deMause, 1976; Fildes, 1988). The emotional truth that is made clear in *Romeo and Juliet* is that the deepest and most significant attachments are made with those who feed and look after us. These two irreconcilable claims still clash within our psychological thinking about nurses and nannies, and serve as a partial explanation for the difficulty there has been in theorizing about them. It has been difficult to accept that the truly loved person might not be the mother or father.

Juliet's nurse was not in a unique position, since the wet nurse had been used by the rich and the poor to feed newborn infants for the past three thousand years (Fildes, 1988). She has ensured the survival of many infants who were orphaned at birth, as in the case of Mohammed. She has been needed to ensure the survival of foundlings such as Oedipus. She has been employed in all the Royal households throughout Europe and parts of the East, and in many rich and aspiring middle classes she has been seen as a necessary status symbol. The history of the wet nurse is a fascinating reminder that the raising of children has relied upon these care-takers, and yet there are few memorials to these women, who, as in the case of Juliet's nurse, sacrificed their own child for the sake of another child who was more privileged. There were a few heart-warming exceptions to the fashion of handing over the feeding of the child to someone other than the mother. For instance, there are two seventeenth-century monuments, one in Edwardstone in Suffolk, and one in Kimbolton in Cambridgeshire, that described two mothers, Elizabeth Brand, who nursed her twelve children with "unborrowed milk", and Lady Essex, who nursed seven of her eight children "with her owne breasts". A more heartbreaking moment took place when Mary Verney was sending her son, Ralph, in 1647, to a wet nurse in the country. She was most anxious that he had a comfortable journey, for, "the child will nott endure to be long out of ones arms" (quoted in Fildes, 1988, pp. 82, 87).

The case of Juliet's wet nurse seems to show that she made an "impression" upon Juliet's psyche. Today, we might describe the nurse as the most important attachment figure in Juliet's life. But whatever way is used to describe the relationship between Juliet and her nurse, Shakespeare brings to our attention that the nurse can be the emotional centre of a child's life. It is for this reason that the nurse must be included in theories of the inner world, and no longer must she be left hovering outside as an "uninvited guest". It might be argued that the wet nurse is a special case, for she must forge a stronger attachment to the child she suckles than a nurse who feeds a child from a bottle. Nevertheless, there seems to be a strong enough case to suggest that whether a child is raised by a wet nurse or a dry nurse, a relationship will be created, for good or for ill, that will leave an "impression" for the rest of life.

By the end of the nineteenth century, certainly in England and in many parts of Europe, the wet nurse had, for the most part, died out. Her demise could be attributed to several facts, one being the philosophical ideas of such Enlightenment writers as Locke and Rousseau, who began to suggest that the early impressions of child-hood have a lasting impact upon the development of character. These ideas gradually affected the child-rearing practices of the middle class, but, at the same time, there was a shift in the working practices of the less privileged. The growth of industry absorbed young women into manufacturing work and they were no longer available as wet nurses, yet, at the same time, wet nursing was no longer the best source of income. But perhaps the shift away from the use of the wet nurse could be attributed to the invention of the bottle in 1869. Infant survival was less dependent on breast milk (Fildes, 1988). The nineteenth century saw this important shift in child-rearing practices, whether the children were rich or poor, but the rich seemed reluctant to give up their belief that "farming out" their children was the best way to bring them up. There followed in England and in other parts of Europe, such as Russia, the rise of the British nanny, though now she would be in the nursery wing of the house (Gathorne-Hardy, 1993).

Fildes, in her history of wet nursing, points out that it "is an occupation which is as old as time" (1988, p. xiv), for the wet nurse ensured the survival of infants, whether privileged or deprived. Therefore, it seems astonishing that she has scarcely been recognized in our cultural history and never appears, except as a shadowy, unexamined figure. One of the striking things when reading about the role of the wet nurse is to discover there were elaborate rules that were laid out about who was suitable to become a wet nurse. These rules were taken from medieval texts from Greece, Rome, and Byzantium, and, summarizing some of these texts, we could say that she needed to be young and to have had a son about two months before, her milk needed to be of good colour, she needed to abstain from all sexual relationship with her husband, and to be careful what she ate. From these elaborate rules, we get a sense that, throughout the history of the wet nurse, there has been a strong undercurrent of anxiety about the effect that the milk of the wet nurse might be having upon the child she was feeding. The rules reflect the uncomfortable knowledge that the milk the wet nurse was giving was involved with the intimacies of her body and her sexuality, and this might affect the identity of the child.

As early as 1235, Henry III had passed a law prohibiting Christian wet nurses suckling Jews, and this legal paranoia summons up a thread of anxiety that runs through all the accounts of wet nurses. What is their milk doing to the child they are suckling? As late as 1864, Margot Asquith, in her Autobiography, writes,

> My second sister, Charlotte . . . was the only member of the family . . . who was tall. My mother attributed this—and her good looks— to her wet nurse, Janet Mercer, a mill-girl noted for her height and beauty. [Gathorne-Hardy, 1993, p. 41]

The attribution of beauty and height to the milk of the wet nurse was a symbolic way of expressing an awareness that a powerful relationship was built up between the child and the wet nurse. Not only might the milk of the wet nurse make her child tall and beautiful, but the child might be changed out of all recognition. Margaret Asquith's mother was reflecting on a "universal belief that the physical and mental characteristics of the nurse were imbibed by the child through her milk" (Fildes, 1988, p. 20). As late as 1887, Freud wrote about the wet nurse they had employed to feed his eldest daughter, Mathilde, in the following way,

> The story of the wet nurse is as follows; she produced less and less milk; at the time she devoured outrageous quantities of everything imaginable; finally she got indigestion, felt miserable, and on top of it all the child developed a *green* stool. [Freud, 1961]

From Gildes' account, the wet nurse did not die out until the end of the nineteenth century, so surely this raises the question as to how many of the early pioneers in psychoanalysis were raised by wet nurses? There seems to be a deathly, or is it shameful, silence? Freud employed a wet nurse for his daughter, Mathilde. Was it possible that Freud's own nurse was a wet nurse, especially as his mother was pregnant with his brother Julius by the time Freud was six or seven months old? Melanie Klein was fed by a wet nurse (Grosskurth, 1985). Bion was born in 1897 and spent his early years in India. He had a beloved Ayah, whom he said he loved more than his mother and whose oriental tales enriched his imagination all his life (Bion, 1982; Bleandonu, 1994). Was she also a wet nurse? In the case of Bowlby, he had the typically deprived childhood of the upper middle class. He lived in a nursery wing that was separated from the rest of the house, and his parents were only seen for an hour every evening. His beloved nurse Minnie left when he was four, and he remained broken-hearted for the rest of his life (Holmes, 1993; Van Dijken, 1998). Bowlby, in 1958, was to write, "For a child to be looked after entirely by a loving nanny and then for her to leave when he is two or three, or even four or five, can be almost as tragic as the loss of the mother" (p. 7). Was Minnie also a wet nurse? Perhaps we shall never know.

Even if Freud's nurse did not breast-feed him, he suffered an emotional struggle to understand her place within his psyche, as the opening quotation shows. He intuitively knew his nurse had left an "impression" upon him, but as he searched for the nature of this impression, it faded under the more forceful imprint of his mother, or, another way of putting it might be to say, she disappeared under the weight of Freud's Oedipal theory. Here is what he wrote to Fliess in 1897 about the strong impression that his Nurse had left upon him. She was "my 'primary originator' [of my hysteria] . . . an ugly, elderly but clever woman who told me a great deal about God and hell, and gave me a high opinion about my own capacities". Freud seems certain in this letter that she had given him a high opinion of himself, for he ended by saying, "If . . . I succeed in resolving my hysteria, I shall have to thank the memory of the old woman who provided me at such an early age with *the means for living and surviving*" (Masson, 1985, pp. 219–220, my italics).

But something significant seems to happen in Freud's thinking. How can he bring together his feeling that his nurse had given him "the means for living and surviving" with the trauma of what happened to her? Freud's nurse was dismissed and sent to prison, by his uncle Philipp, when Freud was two and a half, on what seems like a trumped up charge of having stolen Freud's toys and money. At that time, his mother was in bed having his sister, Anna, and Freud's younger brother Julius had died just six months earlier. Freud had his anchor swept away from him overnight, and in the most traumatic way imaginable. She was sent to prison, or "boxed in" (*ibid.*, pp. 222–223). One can sense in this letter that he is struggling to give an account of this profoundly moving attachment that is suddenly severed. Several psychoanalysts have suggested that this trauma left him without words to describe his pain. He would have been already ridden by guilt following the death of his brother, Julius, whom he would have been unable to mourn; this would then have been compounded by the sudden departure of his nurse. It would have been impossible for Freud to have recognized his sense of betrayal by his mother, so his distress was transformed into an idealization of his mother and his sense of betrayal was transferred to his nurse. In this way, he managed to preserve his mother and neglect the pain that his nurse's dismissal had caused him (Erikson, 1955; Hardin, 1985; Raphael-Leff, 1990).

This shift from the importance of his nurse to the idealized image of his mother becomes clear as Freud develops his Oedipal theory. By 1917, Freud no longer attributes his self-confidence to his relationship with his nurse, but to the special relationship he had had with his mother, as her eldest son. He wrote,

> I have, however, already remarked elsewhere that if a man has been his mother's undisputed darling he retains throughout life the triumphant feeling, the confidence in success, which not seldom brings actual success along with it. [Freud, 1917b, p. 156]

And then, sixteen years later, he added to this idea an even more idealized account of the relationship between a mother and her eldest son. "A mother is brought unlimited satisfaction by her relation to a son; this is altogether the most perfect, the most free from ambivalence of all human relationships" (Freud, 1933a, p. 133).

It would be easy to point the finger of blame at Freud for the sidelining of the nurse in psychoanalytic theory. He got rid of his nurse, as it were, so there has been a tendency to follow in his footsteps and ignore her significance, or to have subsumed her under the generic term of "mother". By subsuming the nurse in this way, her image fades. For instance, Mahler, in 1961, wrote,

> The primitive ego seems to possess an amazing ability to absorb and synthesize complex object images without adverse effect, and on occasion even with benefit. Thus, the Gestalt of the nurse, who may be relegated to the function of providing immediate need satisfaction, is synthesized with the Gestalt of the mother, who may be available only as an additional or transient ego. [p. 334]

Here, Mahler is carrying on the Freudian belief that the *Gestalt* of the nurse becomes the *Gestalt* of the mother, and so the nurse disappears as a person in her own right and her "impression" is effaced, even though, as Mahler says, the nurse may have provided "immediate need satisfaction".

The fading-out of Freud's nurse reflected not only his own unmourned loss, but also the more general cultural anxiety about nurses referred to above. It has been difficult to imagine that the child-rearing pattern of handing over children to others could turn children into strangers and break the emotional bond with the parents. It was even more unthinkable to imagine that the nurse or nanny might be doing harm to the child. Culturally, there has been a need, and Freud was no exception, to believe that parental figures, whatever they do or do not do, are the only significant people in the life of their child.

Gathorne-Hardy, in his book on the British nanny (1993), opens with two accounts of the influence the nanny had upon the child she looked after. Winston Churchill had a Mrs Everest who looked after him tenderly all his childhood. It is also true that he had a wet nurse, and the effect of these two nannies may be reflected in a remark his wife, Lady Churchill, made towards the end of his life, "If it were left to him he'd have two nurses for the rest of his life" (*ibid.*, p. 23) The impression of these two nannies never faded from his mind, though it was Mrs Everest who was loved most passionately. She not only saved his life when he had pneumonia, but she also insisted that he should be taken away from his prep school when she saw the weals the headmaster had inflicted across his back. Not surprisingly, when Mrs Everest died, as has been described, Churchill erected a memorial to his nanny, for, as he wrote, "She had been my dearest and most intimate friend during the whole of the twenty years I had lived" (*ibid.*). Mrs Everest had given Churchill a reason for living.

By contrast, Lord Curzon, who was to become Viceroy of India from 1898 to 1905, had his life deformed by the cruelty he suffered at the hands of his nanny, Miss Paraman. Curzon himself described her in the following way,

> She persecuted and beat us in the most cruel way and established over us a system of terrorism so complete that not one of us ever

mustered up the courage to walk upstairs and tell our father or mother. [Gathorne-Hardy, 1993, p. 17]

Gathorne-Hardy, quite rightly, attributes the characteristics that Curzon developed, such as his obsessive need to control and to overwork, to the "system of terrorism" that Miss Paraman had inflicted upon him as a young child. At the very end of his life, Miss Paraman's treatment of Curzon still echoed within him and he "died embittered, frustrated and unsatisfied, having lost every single one of his friends" (*ibid.*, p. 17). It seems inconceivable, from these accounts, that the "impression" of these two nannies could not be found within the internal world of Churchill and Curzon, for, as Gathorne-Hardy argues, they had shaped their characters and determined much of their later actions.

There has always been an underlying anxiety about the caretaker and the effect she may be having on the child she looks after, as seen above. But this anxiety has not been explored or thought about in our psychological theories. For instance, Hanna Segal, in an interview with Virginia Hunter (1993), said that she had been brought up by innumerable nannies, "who kept changing every few months or every few years" during the first six years of her life, because her mother was "a lady of leisure" who never got out of bed before mid-day. However she does not dwell upon the effect of this child-rearing practice upon her psychic development, she simply comments that this shifting and changing array of nannies had left her with "A depressing streak, not anything damaging" (quoted in Gathorne-Hardy, 1993, p. 306).

"Not anything damaging" might be the best description in the psychoanalytic literature as to the way nannies and nurses have been seen. But there lies something more painful underneath the fact of being brought up by a nanny or a nurse. An estrangement between mother and child can take place, as in the case of Freud, Bion, or Bowlby. If the nurse or nanny is loved or depended upon and she leaves precipitously, the child's heart can be broken and a split may occur in the psyche, leaving a lifelong anxiety about forming another close relationship.

This is well described by Tomlin in her biography of Jane Austen. Jane Austen's mother, in 1776, put Jane into a foster family in the village, when she was probably about fourteen weeks old, and she stayed there for about a year or eighteen months, "until she was old enough to be easily managed at home". The effect this "farming out" had upon Jane, Tomlin suggests, created "the emotional distance between child and mother". Tomlin goes on to say Jane Austen's early experience left her with an uncertainty about "where to expect love or to look for security" (Tomlin, 1997, pp. 6–7). There is no suggestion in Tomlin's account that Jane Austen's mother was being cruel and rejecting. She was following a pattern that we have already seen was common, and, moreover, it seems that she probably visited Jane every day, for the foster family lived in the same village. What Tomlin's account of the upbringing of Jane Austen highlights is that if the child is "farmed out", or has a wet nurse or nanny, and whether rich or poor, an estrangement from the mother takes place. This is what has been so painful to acknowledge, historically, sociologically, and psychologically.

There seem to be three possible pitfalls that can occur when a nurse or nanny is employed as the principal care-taker of the child. If the much loved nurse or nanny leaves prematurely, the child's heart can be broken. There can be a splitting of the psyche between "two mothers". Finally, an estrangement from the parents can take place (Hardin, 1985). There is, however, another significant area that can cause concern, which is the erotic attachment between child and its nurse or nanny.

There is a striking example of how difficult it has been for psychoanalytic theory to gets its mind around the problem of the sexuality of the nurse and her influence upon the sexual development of the child. Freud saw Clarence Oberndorf for a brief and what seems quite acrimonious analysis in Vienna, after the First World War. Oberndorf, in 1958, published his autobiography, describing his early childhood in Alabama. He nearly died at birth, but he writes, "It seems that I remained alive during my first year chiefly because of the devotion of a Negro wet nurse and a conscientious small-town doctor". He then goes on to say that his early memories are coloured "in both senses by the Negroes of the household to whom one habitually resorted for solace and advice". In his first meeting with Freud, he brought a dream in which "I was on the driver's seat of an old-fashioned country wagon drawn by a white horse and a black horse". Freud's interpretation was that

Oberndorf had unconsciously "been under the influence of two fathers, a white father Joe and a black father Joe, our Negro coachman" (Oberndorf, 1958, pp. 8–9). Freud and Oberndorf disagreed over this interpretation and Oberndorf soon left, and it seems Freud was quite dismissive of him (Ginsburg, 1999).

Another story has come down regarding Oberndorf's brief analysis with Freud, and this time it is from Oberndorf's colleague. It is worth noting, for it takes us into a dilemma that is at its most transparent when a white child has had its deepest attachment to a "black Mammy". The story goes that Oberndorf and Freud fell out over the dream because Freud had told Oberndorf that he would never marry because he could not make up his mind whether to choose a black woman or a white woman (Kardiner, 1977). Oberndorf never married.

This anecdote helps to confirm the impression that Freud made an astute observation about the sexual conflict that can be set up by having "two mothers", a black mother and a white mother, especially in a country where racial segregation was enforced. However, Freud's Oedipal theory has made it difficult to reconcile the observation that Oberndorf had a black woman and a white woman in his internal world. It is generally held to be true that, within the structure of the psyche, there is to be found only one mother and one father and—perhaps we should add—they are white.

This is not the place to get into the racial and political difficulties that have followed Western colonization and the employment of slaves and indigenous natives to help raise the children of white colonists. But, in the case of Oberndorf, in his internal world he had "two mothers", one of whom was black and believed to be racially and socially inferior. His heartbreak and conflict was that his society forbade him to recognize his erotic feelings for black women that were linked to his deep love and gratitude to his "black Mammy", who had not only saved his life, but might have, as with Freud, given him a reason for living.

To return briefly to Freud's early correspondence with Fliess, already mentioned, we get something of this erotic dilemma as Freud describes his feelings about his nurse. He first of all calls her "my 'primary originator' [of my hysteria]", but then he goes on and writes that she was "my instructress in sexual matters" (Masson, 1985, pp. 219–220). In other words, Freud was struggling to understand the effect she may have had upon his sexual identity and fantasies. The erotic attachment to the nurse or nanny goes to the heart of the difficulty that has always attended the handing over of the child to another to raise. She might become the internal model for later love relationships.

Hardin has written extensively on what he calls the "surrogate mother" and the effect that she can have upon psychic development (Hardin, 1985). The reason the "surrogate mother" has been ignored is that the pain she causes when she leaves gets repressed. However, her voice can be heard when the real mother is described as cold and distant or idealized. Paradoxically, this "surrogate mother" is most fully present in the psyche when she has left and a hole in the heart of the child has been created. There are certain general characteristics that can be observed of a child reared by a "surrogate mother" who leaves. A child who is primarily looked after by a "surrogate mother" necessarily becomes alienated from the mother. This alienation can be reflected in the therapy and repeated in the transference, with the therapist being kept at arm's length. But the cold relationship within the therapy could give a clue to a warmer relationship that has been buried and forgotten.

The loss of the "surrogate mother" can cripple the child's capacity to form a lasting or close relationship in adult life. The child in adult life can find him/herself pursuing a love affair with someone who always leaves them, thus perpetuating the original trauma of the lost "surrogate mother". Hardin observes that with the loss of the "surrogate mother" in the early life of the child, she becomes hidden behind "screen memories" or dreams of the mother, such as we saw with Freud's struggle with the "impression" of his nurse. For some, who have a cold and distant relationship with their mother, they may be hiding a grief for a much loved "surrogate mother" who left.

In conclusion, wet nurses, nannies, and nurses are curiously absent in most psychological theories on emotional development. This absence must reflect a general cultural belief that the nurse is only a "servant" who can be dismissed at any time, thus reinforcing the idea that the parents hold the reins of power. This cultural wish has obscured the emotional truth that when children are handed over to someone else to bring up, they might become alienated from their parents. In some cases, the child could suffer irreparable pain, either at the hands of the nurse or if the nurse leaves prematurely. It is only when parents recognize that they may be creating a distance with their child when they hand him or her over to another that they might be more willing to recognize that the nurse might have become more important to the child's wellbeing than they are.

The idealization of the role of the mother and the ignoring of the significance of the nurse or nanny is reflected in Freud's theory, but also within social and cultural history. In so doing, there has been an avoidance of thinking about a possible twofold inner devastation. The child might feel betrayed by the mother who hands her/him over to be cared for by another, and another devastation may occur if the nurse or nanny leaves prematurely.

The nurse or nanny's metaphorical portrait needs to be brought out and dusted down, so that she can be hung in the gallery alongside the parents, grandparents, siblings, and other ancestors who have been considered in previous chapters. It is time she was remembered for the impossible role she has been placed in, rather than considered as no more than a "servant" who can be fired and hired at the whim of the mistress. It needs to be recognized that a blind eye has been turned to the fact that the nurse often has been given the vital task of caring for a child at its most vulnerable and impressionable age.

When there has been a cruel nanny (and it as an open question as to where that portrait should be hung, such as Miss Paraman), she serves to highlight an endemic gap that is created when parents hand over the care of a child to a nurse or nanny. As Curzon said, "not one of us ever mustered up the courage to walk upstairs and tell our father or mother". This lack of courage may be the result of Miss Paraman's sadistic cruelty, but may reflect the distance and alienation that is created when children are looked after by others. In many cases, there may be no symbolic stairs to climb to reach back to their parents. The failure to recognize the significance of the nurse or nanny has been one of the unwritten tragedies that stalks unbidden and without words through our psychological theories. It is time she was mourned if she left prematurely; as she is remembered, the meaning of the early emotional life and fantasies of the child will cease to be attributed solely to the relationship with parents.

CHAPTER SIX

The trauma of war

"Yet once I discovered this unexplained suicide [of my great grandmother], I came to see it as a symbol that spoke for three generations of my family"

(Holroyd, 2010, p. 323)

I n the previous chapters, it has been argued that to know of the ancestral past may be an important part in unlocking a repetitive and destructive pattern of behaviour. Orestes was caught up in three generations of violent revenge. Oedipus was blighted by the deceptions that accompanied his unwanted birth. In the clinical cases of Martha, Muriel, and Nicholas, they all carried an ancestral history that was painfully discovered. The work that has been done since the 1960s on the legacy of the Second World War, and, in particular, the help that has been given to the survivors of the Holocaust and their children, shows most clearly the way traumatic experience rebounds on the second and third generation.

The work of several analysts, mostly working in the USA, in the late 1970s and in the 1980s with survivors of the Holocaust made it more possible to think about the way in which traumatic experiences of parents can be transmitted to their children (Berg-man & Jucovy, 1982; Kestenberg & Kestenberg, 1982; Krystal, 1978; Niederland, 1968a). In the collection of essays that were brought together in *Generations of the Holocaust* (Bergman & Jucovy, 1982), there was general agreement that there had been a collective "wall of silence" from analysts, psychiatrists, doctors, and the general population about the aftermath of the Second World War, and, in particular, there had been a denial of the effect of the Holocaust on survivors and their children (Bergman & Jucovy, 1982, p. 33). It had needed twenty years after the ending of the war before the helping professions began to be aware that there had been a neglect of this historical fact. For instance, patients were returning to therapy after an earlier analysis that had ignored the Holocaust as a meaningful event in the inner world. The failure to think about the psycholog-ical effects of the Holocaust was partly to do with what was called a "latency period", which was defined as the time it took for analysts to face and find a language to express the horror of what had happened (Kestenberg, 1975; Kestenberg & Kestenberg, 1982).

It could be said that to call this period of silence a necessary "latency period" was being too generous towards the psychiatrists, psychotherapists, and psychoanalysts who had greeted the sur-vivors of the Holocaust. Some felt that there had been a conspiracy of silence due to the countertransference reactions of rage and guilt in the professionals (Danielli, 1984). This divided response to the silence that greeted the returning survivors is echoed in the differ-ing reactions of survivors themselves. Some survivors felt that they needed time to process their experiences within themselves before they could speak, and their therapists recognized that in talking too soon there was a danger that they would be retraumatized further. For instance, Buergenthal, writing his memoirs *Lucky Child* in 2010, said he could only write of his experiences sixty years after his survival in Auschwitz, Sachsenhausen, and the ghetto of Kiele, for, he maintained that

> Had I written this book in the mid-eighties, when . . . I could still
> vividly recall my fear of dying, the hunger I experienced, the sense
> of loss and insecurity that gripped me on being separated from my
> parents and my reactions to the horrors I witnessed . . . I would
> have found it difficult, if not impossible, to overcome my past

without serious psychological scarring. It may have been my salvation that these memories faded over time. [Buergenthal, 2010, pp. xxii–xxiii]

In contrast, others desperately needed to be listened to and understood, and when they were met with disbelief and distrust, this added to their trauma (Danielli, 1984; Wiesel, 1970). Primo Levi, on returning from Auschwitz, managed to break through the silence that greeted survivors by talking and talking to anyone who would listen to him, and this continued for about two years (Angier, 2002). At the same time, he was writing a remarkable account of how he managed to survive the Holocaust (Levi, 1958). He had realized, within the first two weeks of arriving in Auschwitz, that his psychological survival in the camp depended upon recording and trying to make sense of the Inferno that he found himself in. So, while there might not be a right or wrong way, as therapists, to respond to those who have survived a severe trauma, it was gradually realized that the failure to acknowledged the historical reality of the survivors' experience could be felt as a damaging failure of empathy.

As the accounts of survivors filtered through into both the public sphere and into the consulting rooms of psychotherapy, it became clear that not all those survivors who were distressed necessarily had a previous history of earlier infantile conflict (Jucovy, 1992). This caused a certain conflict within orthodox psychoanalytic belief and might help to explain why the Holocaust experience was unexamined. It was generally thought to be true that "External events, no matter how overwhelming, precipitate a neurosis only when they touch on specific unconscious conflicts" (Zetzel, 1970, p. 183). It was gradually being recognized that this view imprisoned the capacity of therapists to think that the Holocaust was an event that had stretched human understanding as never before. For instance, Primo Levi brought to the attention of the civilized world that Dante's Inferno had stepped off the pages of literary imagination and become reality in Auschwitz and other extermination camps. But it took time, in the first place, for the professionals to recognize that the Holocaust had inflicted a unique and unheard-of suffering that had blown the psyche apart and, second, to realize that it was insulting to the survivors to attribute their pain to their upbringing. The Freudian conflict model of the mind that based psychic structure upon unacceptable sexual wishes that had to be repressed was gradually being replaced with a view that the mind can be blown apart by extreme trauma and, therefore, conflict resolution was not the way to help those who had a "hole in the mind" (Cohen, 1980).

The shock of realizing that the Holocaust had traumatized adult minds in ways that had never been seen before was compounded by the realization that the children of survivors were also traumatized. And here, the collective silence of the psychoanalytic community carried a more general cultural reluctance to accept that a trauma might have consequences that could damage the second and even the third generation. The idea that trauma might be carried across generations brings into sharper focus a belief expressed in the Old Testament that the sins of the forefathers are visited unto the third and fourth generation (Deuteronomy, 5.9, Holy Bible). This belief runs counter to ideas of the Enlightenment, in which self-knowledge is seen as a tool to emancipate man from his irrational emotions and help him to determine his future more freely. In so far as psychoanalytic understanding is a child of the Enlightenment, it is not surprising that the focus of psychoanalytic attention has been upon the individual's way of experiencing the world. The teasing out of the unique qualities that make up each person's emotional life has enriched our imagination and our understanding of the mind of man immeasurably. But it has meant that the historical and generational patterns of behaviour within the family have not received as much attention as the individual's early childhood experience.

Once it was realized, within the psychoanalytic community, that there had been a failure to acknowledge the enormity of the suffering of the returning survivors, there was a significant shift in the position that therapists took in understanding psychic trauma. "The Group for the Psychoanalytic Study of the Effect of the Holocaust on the Second Generation" was formed in 1974 by Kestenberg, who collated the work of analysts from the USA, Israel, Germany, and Canada. It became increasingly clear that the "second generation" children, who were being presented in child guidance clinics, were deeply disturbed by the earlier history of the parents' traumatic experiences. And so it became more generally accepted that these children needed to know the historical facts of the Holocaust and of the terrible losses their parents had experienced. "It is only to the extent that historical reality is ascertained that the patient will be able to approach his own inner and outer reality" (Grubrich-Simitis, 1981, p. 440). Those children, who were helped to see that they were carrying many of the complex feelings that the parents could not metabolize, became freer to lead more creative lives.

The seemingly sensible task of helping the survivors "mourn" their losses met another phenomenon that ran contrary to another deeply held psychoanalytic belief about mourning, which is that death could be "got over". "[W]hen the work of mourning is completed the ego becomes free and uninhibited again" (Freud, 1917e, p. 245). However, the more stable social world that had influenced Freud's thinking had been overturned by the Holocaust. Whole families of several generations were wiped out, and, as a result, therapists were forced to conclude that the experience of the Holocaust had been so traumatic that in some cases it had created "a hole in the mind" (Cohen, 1980) and, hence, there were "irreversible and even progressive mental changes which may resist any treatment" (Winnick, 1968, p. 298). It was disquieting to discover that some traumatic events could not be mourned and got over in the way that Freud had suggested. New ways needed to be found to contain and stay with the painful knowledge that, in some cases, the Holocaust experience had created irremediable psychic damage.

It seems clear that the work that has been done with Holocaust survivors and their children has changed the landscape of psychoanalytic thinking and brought up again for reconsideration one of the founding tenets of psychoanalysis, which is that mental distress has its roots in early trauma. The difficulty that Freud's two concepts of trauma, the traumatic situation and the overwhelming affects, has caused much debate within psychoanalytic theory (Grubrich-Simitis, 1981; Sandler, Dreher & Drews, 1991). Krystal (1978) took the view that Freud's two concepts are not contradictory if we distinguish between trauma that occurs in childhood and trauma that occurs when adult. The acceptance of these two concepts allowed Krystal to move to a distinction between the psychic trauma of the Holocaust, when experienced in adult life, and the experience of trauma in early infancy. For example, in the case of an infant who is left alone in a distressed state for too long, it is traumatized by the feelings that overwhelm it because the child has not developed a capacity to contain the emotions. It is utterly dependent upon adult care-takers to relieve its distress. By contrast, in the adult, it is not the feelings that overwhelm, but "it is the over-whelming of the ego, the surrender in total helplessness and hope-lessness, and the progression to the catanoid state that makes the situation traumatic". Krystal stressed that adult psychic trauma is never the same as the "*timeless* horror" of an infant left in a word-less state of unbearable distress: ". . . this kind of experience is the most terrible and describable hell known to man, literally a fate worse than death". An adult who is traumatized for any length of time by a world gone mad is affected in a different way, because the adult has developed an ego with "self observing functions" (*ibid.*, pp. 97–101).

There is, however, one difficulty that arises from Krystal's distinction between adult and infant trauma, which is that the distinction seems to collapse when the behavioural symptoms are observed. An infant left to cry too long becomes silent and falls asleep. The adult in the unbearable situation of a concentration camp becomes numb and depersonalized. The traumatized infant cuts himself off from feeling pain or joy. Similarly, the traumatized adult becomes depressed and withdrawn from contact. So, although Kyrstal's separation of adult trauma from infantile trauma seems to make intuitive sense, it might be difficult to bear in mind this distinction when confronted by a traumatized adult who might be living in a joyless world.

Nevertheless, Krystal's distinction between infant and adult trauma could be helpful in thinking about a question as to how parents transmit their suffering to their children (Herzog, 1982). Herzog asks,

> How does what the parents endured or escaped make its way into the mind of the child? Are the modes of transmission conscious or unconscious and intentional, or do they occur through the uncon-scious channel? Can a general model for the transmission of trauma be constructed? [*ibid.*, p. 103]

It could be said that what escapes into the mind of the child is the parents' state of mind, and it is in this way that the adult survivor, unwittingly and unconsciously, traumatizes his child in infancy. For instance, the child may arouse extreme anxiety and hatred in the parents if he is difficult or wants to be independent. The parents' anxious fantasies that the child does not love them or wants to abandon them lead them to act with unwitting cruelty towards their child. The child can be called "a little Hitler", or even have its head put in an oven, thus inflicting an infantile trauma (Kestenberg & Kestenberg, 1982). So, a first step in constructing a general model for the transmission of trauma might be to suggest that it is through the traumatizing of infants by their traumatized parent that the cycle of intergenerational trauma continues.

The idea that we need to look at child-rearing practices to understand how the parents' trauma is transmitted to the next generation has been developed in many studies on attachment (Bowlby, 1969; Fonagy, Steele, Moran, Steele, & Higgitt, 1991; Fraiberg, 1982; Main & Hesse, 1990). On this account, the transmission takes place through the way the mother responds to her newborn child. If the mother has suffered severe trauma, she might be unable to function well enough. Many newly liberated mothers were extremely anxious and distressed and often failed to manage their infants' emotional responses. These mothers could not contain or protect their children from unbearable feelings for they, in turn, could feel threatened by the emotional growth of their child and attacked if their child was angry or difficult. In many cases, they were longing for the child to provide them with the mothering they had lost. It seems clear that the early experience of many women who had survived the adult trauma of the Holocaust, unwittingly traumatized their infants by their difficulty in containing their infant's passions (Grubrich-Simitis, 1981).

Another result of early maternal failure was that the children of Holocaust survivors began to turn up in the child guidance clinics around the world, displaying a set of symptoms that matched the parent's disturbances. It was beginning to become clear that these traumatized children seemed to have identified with the parents manifold suffering and this, in turn, led them to inhabit what was termed the "survivor syndrome" (Niederland, 1968a). The concept of the "survivor syndrome" carries complex characteristics for both parents and children. The parents experience guilt that they have survived, but they also experience anger with those members of the family who have died. These feelings are mixed with contempt for those who failed to survive. It seemed that these difficult feelings were passed on to their children in an undigested and unprocessed way, so that the children suffered the same type of "survivor syndrome" symptoms of guilt, anger, and contempt, though these symptoms were reflected in somatic anxieties, depression, and separation anxiety. What was, however, unique to the children was that many of them had also unconsciously identified with their dead grandparents, often through being given their name. This identification carried a difficult twist or "double bind" (Bateson, 1972), for these children were hated for reminding their parents of their lost and "abandoning" parents—the children's grandparents—while, at the same time, the children unconsciously imagined or hoped that by becoming like the grandparents their parents would be comforted and their suffering could be brought to an end (Kogan, 1992).

The unconscious hatred that these children aroused in their parents for reminding them of their lost families was compounded by another destructive factor. In many cases, the parents had unconsciously identified with their persecutors in the concentration camps, and unknowingly, as it were, they would treat their children as though they had become the persecutors if the children tried to assert their independence. As has already been said, it was not unknown for parents to call their children "Little Hitler" and in some cases actually put their children's head in the oven. It seemed that the

> repetition of the trauma in relation to the children may be bound
> by two factors: identification with the parents' own parents, who
> "abandoned" them, and identification with the persecutors, who
> become the authorities in lieu of the degraded and killed parents.
> [Kestenberg & Kestenberg, 1982, p. 44]

To illustrate some of the complex emotions that parents and children suffered as a consequence of the Holocaust, Kestenberg (1980) cites a case of unconscious cruelty that two Holocaust survivors inflicted upon their son. She describes his desperate attempt to restore his parents. Marvin went into therapy in his late adolescence, feeling that he and the rest of the world were worthless "dirt". His mother had survived Auschwitz, but had lost all her family, including her husband and children. His father had also lost his wife and children in the genocide. Mother and father were middle-aged when they met, and Marvin was their only child. This child was expected to be "a child of hope, of resurrection, and a repudiation of Hitler's genocide". However, far from Marvin helping his parents to regain hope and belief in the goodness of the world, Marvin became "the personification of evil". He was constantly told that he was not as good as his dead siblings. His father told him he should have been killed when he was four—this was the age of the father's oldest child when he was killed—and the mother wanted to place him in a home because "he was a 'Hitler'" (*ibid.*, p. 778)

This harrowing account of the generational suffering that was the legacy of the Holocaust leaves open the question as to how many generations of unconscious pain will continue if children whose parents have been severely traumatized are not helped to recognize that they are carrying a double burden of their own suffering which is a consequence of their parents' trauma. Another question arises as to whether genocide presents any theory of trauma with unique difficulties about how to stay alongside the damage done to hope. It seems clear from the case of Marvin that he was put into an impossible "double bind". On the one hand, he was expected to carry the hope of the future generation, but, on the other hand, his very liveliness and separateness carried a threat that the parents would be left with unbearable pain and guilt. This "double bind" became particularly unbearable as Marvin approached adolescence with the burgeoning of sexual hopes and desires. Like many other adolescent children of Holocaust survivors, he found himself caught up in multiple identifications with his dead relations and recriminations from his parents that he was not the one who should have survived. One result that was found in many adolescent cases was that their sexual desires were distorted by violent sexual fantasies in which the parents were believed to have colluded sexually with their Nazi captors (Oliner, 1982).

It has already been seen that the children of adult survivors of the Holocaust seem to mimic the "survivor syndrome" symptoms of their parents, with feelings of guilt, anger, and contempt. Another striking feature in the children's suffering was the parallels in their fantasy life with that of their parents. For instance, some of these children, born after the war, reported nightmares about Nazi guards and concentration camps and would re-enact scenes from the parents' past, even though the parents had remained silent and they had no conscious knowledge of these experiences. They seemed to share the same psychic disturbances as their parents (Brody, 1973; Herzog, 1982; Kestenberg, 1980; Kogan, 1992).

Severely traumatized parents will inevitably pass on unconsciously something of their earlier suffering, as the work on the children of Holocaust survivors has shown. One way in which this transmission takes place is through the parents traumatizing their children in infancy and, as a result, the traumatized infant in turn displays some of the characteristic of the parents, even having fantasies about the concentration camps and believing, like Marvin, that they are "dirt". This is why it is so crucial that the children of traumatized adults receive some help in understanding the historical legacy of suffering that they have been unwittingly asked to bear.

Another question that is raised by the work done with Holocaust survivors and their children is whether genocide presents any psychological theory of trauma with unique difficulties about how to stay alongside the damage done to hope. Or, put another way, does genocide present any psychological theory with the painful awareness that some experiences cannot be got over or mourned, as Freud had hoped?

The twentieth-century Armenian painter Arshile Gorky was traumatized by the Armenian genocide of 1915. He and all his family had fled the town of Van, in Eastern Turkey, and marched for weeks to safety in Erevan. There, his mother died in his arms, and Gorky, aged fifteen, and his sister, Vartoosh, aged thirteen, were left as orphans. They were sent to the USA to join up with their father, who had left them many years earlier, to avoid conscription into the Turkish army. Two of Gorky's greatest paintings were of *The Artist and his Mother*. Not only were they unique, for no other artist has painted himself with his mother, but he seemed to have the artistic capacity to give painterly form to an intricate and delicate account of his feelings about his mother, her death during the genocide, and his relationship to her. He seemed able to give expression to his deepest and most passionate feelings in relationship to another, and on this account, he might be said to have achieved a remarkable inner state of integration (Coles, 1990).

Gorky seemed to exemplify Freud's belief that "when the work of mourning is completed the ego becomes free and uninhibited again" (Freud, 1917e, p. 245). Yet Gorky, at the height of his power, killed himself. On the one hand, Gorky had created some of the most original paintings in the twentieth century, and yet, in spite of the exquisite balance he was able to achieve in some of his last paintings, he hanged himself.

His suicide could be explained in terms of the "cumulative trauma" of cancer, a car accident that broke his shoulder so that he could not paint, a fire that burnt down his studio and destroyed twenty paintings, and the death of his estranged father (Khan, 1963). However, the concept of "cumulative trauma" does not actually explain trauma (Krystal, 1978). In the light of the work that has been accumulated on the effects of the Holocaust, Gorky's suicide might be better explained in terms of the psychic devastation done to his mind following the Armenian genocide in which his mother had died in his arms. It was not that Gorky had failed to mourn the death of his mother, but this was not enough to heal his internal devastation that had followed the genocide. Gorky's whole life as a child growing up in Eastern Turkey had been destroyed, and he and his sister had been left homeless and orphaned.

A similar question about the effect of genocide was raised by Gerson in a recent article (2009). Gerson suggests that in genocide the individual is caught up in a social world gone mad in which all safe external structures break down. This creates lasting damage to individual psychic structures and so, for survivors and those who work with them, there has to be a recognition that within the internal world there is what Gerson calls a "dead third", or "a world constituted by absence". His definition of the concept of the "dead third" is "the loss of a 'live third' upon whom the individual previously relied, had entrusted with faith, and in relation to whom or which, had developed a sense of continuity and meaning" (ibid., p. 1343).

From Gerson's generalization about a genocide creating "a world constituted by absence", he moves to consider the life and work of Primo Levi, and, in particular, a late poem called "Unfinished Business". Gerson had had disquieting thoughts about how to understand the suicide of Primo Levi, who had survived Auschwitz. In "Unfinished Business", "the narrator offers his 'resignation' from a life that is experienced as filled with 'uncompleted work'". And Gerson concluded that Levi was expressing his despair that his literary works, and this poem in particular, could not create "a memorial that would . . . repair the trauma of the past by insulating the future from the possibility of a repetition of unbearable atrocity" (*ibid.*, p. 1351). In other words, there had been a failure of mourning. Gerson then had second thoughts. To say of Levi, that he had failed to mourn and, therefore, become melancholic and suicidal, was to commit an act of hubris. How could Levi "get over" the extermination of life that he had witnessed? Maybe, Gerson muses, what Levi has shown us is that "psychological survival requires that the impossibility of life be spoken" (*ibid.*).

It is not quite clear what Gerson means by "psychological survival requires that the impossibility of life be spoken". In one of Gorky's last paintings, called *Summation* (which is in the Museum of Modern Art, New York), painted in the last summer of his life, it feels as though he had brought together in this abstract painting the amorphous forms that had haunted all his work and these "hauntings" had been held together in this work of beauty and harmony. Like Levi's poem, it is finished. But now, as Gerson remarks about Levi's poem, perhaps Gorky's painting "is the creative expression of the failure of creativity to erase destruction" (Angier, 2002), and it is this fact that led him to suicide, not a failure to work through mourning.

However, it is not an entirely satisfying explanation that Levi and Gorky's suicide are linked to their recognition of, "the failure of creativity to erase destruction". This may offer some understanding of why extreme trauma, such as genocide, can undermine psychic structure in the face of meaningless destruction. But something more needs to be taken into account concerning Levi and Gorky's suicide in the light of the work done on the traumatic effects of the Holocaust on subsequent generations. Both men killed themselves when they were in a lot of physical distress. Gorky had bowel cancer that necessitated a bag, and Levi had been investigated for prostate cancer, and this also had required a bag. The disintegration of their bodies had resurrected memories of earlier helplessness.

It would be tempting to equate earlier helplessness with infantile trauma that they had both suffered, for we do know that Levi had suffered depression all his life, and that Gorky lived under an invented identity. But Levi and Gorky were carrying a family history of suffering, for they were part of a persecuted minority, Levi as a Jew in Italy, Gorky as an Armenian in Turkey. They not only carried a historical legacy of racial prejudice, but they also witnessed the difficulties that this prejudice had upon their families. Levi's mother cut herself off from her husband; Gorky's father left the family when Gorky was a child, in order to avoid conscription into the Turkish army. As in the case of Marvin, above, these two great creative artists were carrying the fantasy that they could rescue their families of origin from the hatred that they had all experienced. But when their bodies began to fail them they were ineluctably led to realize that their creative wishes to save their family from its suffering could not be sustained. And with the destruction of their deepest wish, they chose to end their lives. Levi did not leave a suicide note, but Gorky's eloquent note read, "Goodbye Beloveds".

So, where does this leave the question as to whether genocide confronts our psychological theories with the painful awareness that some experiences cannot be got over or mourned, as Freud hoped? In the brief accounts of Gorky and Levi, their suicides take place in spite of their creative capacity. Any explanation of the reason for their suicide needs to take into account the history of their family and race. The "hole in the mind" that can be created by genocide cannot be filled, but, as the work of those who have worked with Holocaust survivors and their children has shown us, some measure of relief can be gained, especially for the second and third generation, by understanding that they are carrying the suffering of their families past history as well as their own. Whether this knowledge would have saved Gorky and Levi cannot be known. However, Levi is reported to have said after his return from Auschwitz, "If you stop up my mouth I die" (Angier, 2002, p. 656). Therefore, as therapists, we must not stop up their mouths with our silence and, most importantly, we need to remember that part of who we are, as Judith Butler so pertinently said, are "enigmatic traces of others" (2004, p. 96).

CHAPTER SEVEN

Brain development and trauma

"In every nursery there are ghosts. They are the visitors from the unremembered past of the parents; the uninvited guests at the christening . . ."

(Fraiberg, 1987, p. 100)

Fraiberg's famous paper stretches the imagination back into the nursery of childhood with the uninvited guests of dead siblings, forgotten grandparents, abandoning parents, and unremembered nannies and nurses, and invites them to the adult table of psychoanalytic discourse. Her paper imagines the position of the child within the nursery and believes that the destructive visitors are from "the unremembered past of the parents". Her therapeutic task with her co-workers, Edna Adelson and Vivian Shapiro, was to try to open up the unremembered past of young mothers who were repeating their childhood trauma of deprivation and abuse upon their own infants. She discovered that however disturbed the mother might seem to be, if she could be helped to remember her own past experience of abuse, she was more able to give up the unconsciously inflicted abuse upon her child. The disturbed mother who had repressed her abuse and cut herself off from her pain by denying any feeling was more likely to identify with the original aggressor and harm her child. The capacity to remember and feel again the original trauma opened up the possibility of changing the abusive legacy of the nursery.

Fraiberg's profound understanding of trauma and its legacy across the generations leads, in this last chapter, to the task of gathering up the various threads that have been explored throughout this book. It is in the patterns of child-rearing that the legacy of ancestral history can impinge upon our psychological freedom and distort our moral judgements. The fantasies and anxieties that are experienced in the nursery in the arms of mothers and care-takers are internalized and lay the foundation for the way future relationships are played out. Put in its most simplistic way, anxious mothers can create anxious babies, who, in turn, become anxious parents. It is people like Fraiberg who have shown the way that abused mothers can repeat their abuse, unwittingly, upon their children, and, as her work points out, one of the most effective ways of preventing the repeating cycle of distress and cruelty is to intervene early. Graham Allen, Labour MP, has written a commissioned Government report into the need for early intervention programmes for young children. He proposes establishing an Early Intervention Foundation aimed at "breaking intractable intergenerational problems" and focusing on the first three years of life. "Nought to three is the really explosive bit of brain growth. If you can help at that point, it is so much more affective, [and] so much cheaper than at any other time" (Allen, 2011). In other words, what Fraiberg's work has helped to show is that the earliest interaction between mother and infant holds the clue to repeating trauma.

The idea that the earliest intersubjective experience between mother and child held the clue to later patterns of relating was already being confirmed in the work done with the survivors of the Holocaust described in the last chapter. The work of pioneers such as Kestenberg brought to psychoanalytic theory a startling perspective upon the way extreme trauma rebounds across several generations. After the Second World War and the unimaginable suffering that was inflicted, the psychoanalytic world seemed to wake from its anti-historical slumber. The historical consequences of trauma could no longer be denied and individual conflict began to be seen within the legacy of generational suffering. The children of trau-matized parents needed help to understand the unconscious know-ledge they had carried of their parents' pain, guilt, and anger. It became clear that the children of survivors could identify with their parents' suffering and carry fantasies that they could take the place of the lost generation. Some children would go to extraordinary lengths to rescue their parents from the agonized denial of pain. In other cases, the children's compulsive actions seemed to be the desperate attempt to make known the secret pain of parents or grandparents and restore lost loved ones. The complex ways trauma eats into the soul became more apparent (Balint, 1993; Faimberg, 2005; Kestenberg, 1972; Kogan, 1992, Rosenfeld, 2006).

The clinical work with Martha (Chapter One), Muriel (Chapter Three), and Nicholas (Chapter Four) revealed their generational tragedy. Through the gradual creation of a narrative to contain the trauma, there was a lessening of the unconscious imprisonment they felt. The unconscious repetition of self-destruction diminished and it became less likely that they would need to inflict their suffer-ing upon their children if and when they had them. It is clear that if any trauma is buried or denied, it needs to be looked for and the unmourned grave disinterred, whether of dead sibling or parent, grandparent, or nanny. This idea was vividly elaborated in the work of Davoine & Gaudillière on the legacy of war (Chapter Three).

The paradigm of generational suffering, seen in the work of Aeschylus (Chapter One) and Sophocles (Chapter Two), made clear that the trauma of family feuds and the abandonment of children eats into the heart of culture and civilization and what starts as a personal tragedy can, in turn, fuel war and social destruction. The chilling worlds of the children of Agamemnon and of Oedipus lead to the recognition that three thousand years of child-rearing prac-tices have, for the most part, ignored the emotional life of the infant. Shakespeare's tragedy of *Romeo and Juliet* was a good case in point, for Juliet was a mere pawn in her parents' lives (Chapter Five). The cruelty inflicted upon children from the earliest records, and the rampant disregard for infant suffering, whether their feet were being bound in China, or they were being dumped at the door of orphanages, such as the children of Rousseau, is a reminder that it is only in the last hundred and fifty years that the mind of the child has been considered (Boswell, 1988; deMause, 1976; Fildes, 1988; Gathorne-Hardy, 1993).

The shift that has taken place in thinking about the infant mind is, in many ways, due to Freud and the developing psychoanalytic theory that adult conflict has its roots in infancy. Much of this book has been about the suffering that man inflicts upon himself and others through a failure to recognize that trauma distorts the emotional responses to life and the structure of the psyche. Nevertheless, the research that is being done on the infant mind, not only within psychoanalysis, but in neurology and biology, is a hopeful reminder that there is no more important work than the nurturing of the next generation.

The work of Krystal, mentioned in the previous chapter, in which he differentiated between infant trauma and adult trauma, has made an important contribution to research into the infant mind. He wrote of "the timeless horror" of an infant left alone in distress, and went on to emphasize that "this kind of experience is the most terrible and indescribable hell known to man, literally a fate worse than death" (Krystal, 1978, p. 97). If one stops for a moment and imagines a newborn infant left in distress for too long, what recourse does it have? It can only give up and turn away, like Nicholas, who was put out of earshot as an infant (see Chapter Four), for at that moment the most imperative need is to survive physically. (It was only in 1889 that a bill was passed in Parliament to protect children from cruelty, but this bill was prompted by the outrage that a bill had already been presented for The Prevention of Cruelty to Animals (see Fildes, 1988; Robertson, 1976, p. 207).) Nicholas's mind would go a blank if he became distressed in adult life, and then, as our work continued and he could trust me a bit more, he began to experience again the timeless horror of nothingness, or the proverbial "black hole", and he feared I was sending him mad.

The work of neurologists, such as Schore and Panksepp, has given new insight into several conflicting states of mind that I experienced with Nicholas. For instance, I was puzzled by the state of arousal that I felt when Nicholas told me that he had been put out of earshot so that his cries could not disturb his father. I felt it again when I read Krystal's work about infants left in "a wordless state of unbearable distress". It seems from the work of neurology that the

right side of my brain was being aroused when I heard those dis-
tressing tales, in much the same way as any mother's brain is aroused
when her infant cries for help (Panksepp & Smith Pasqualini, 2005;
Schore, 2002). Why does knowing about the physiology of the brain
help therapeutically when confronted with someone like Nicholas?

The combined insights from neurological research, biology, and
the two-person psychology of attachment has enlarged the understanding of human suffering and its roots in infancy. Attachment
theory makes intuitive sense that our most imperative need at birth
is the biological necessity to survive. Bowlby had observed the
excruciating suffering of children separated for too long from their
parents, and he was led to the conclusion that this anguish was
stimulated by their fear that they would not survive (Gerhardt,
2005; Schore, 2002). He believed this observation was confirmed by
the earlier ethological studies of Lorenz (1935) on the biological
necessity of animals to form a strong attachment to their mothers
(Bowlby, 1969). Bowlby's theory of the psychological importance
of attachment led to empirical research into observations about
the way infants attach themselves to their parents. This led to the
realization that the newborn infant has not only a need, but the
capacity, to form a relationship at birth with its care-taker (Jones,
2006; Murray, 1992; Schore, 2002; Stern, 1985; Trevarthen, 2008).
This relational need, which Bowlby had already suggested was
primarily occasioned by the biological need to survive, connects
with all mammalian life.

It seems to be generally accepted that our brain has evolved
through three stages. There is the earliest reptilian brain, "an ancient amphibian reptilian toolshed at its core", at the base of the brain
(Jones, 2006; Murray, 1992; Schore, 2002; Stern, 1985; Trevarthen,
2008). Then there is the mammalian emotional brain in the brain
stem, which connects to the autonomic nervous system and
includes the amygdala, the hippocampus, and the orbito-frontal
cortex. Around and above the right hemisphere of the brain develops the prefrontal cortex and cingulate, and, as it grows during the
first three years of infancy, so does the capacity to speak, symbol-
ize, think, and reflect upon the self and others (Morrison, 1999, cited
in Gerhardt, 2005, p. 34).

The work that has been done upon the biology of the infant has
shown the way in which, from the earliest days of infancy, the right

brain regulates the body and responds to the external environment (Gerhardt, 2005; Schore, 2002). It has become incontrovertible that the infant cannot regulate its own body without the help of the mother or care-taker. And it is this observation about the two-way feedback between infant and mother that has shifted, in many subtle ways, how we think about children and the way psycho-analysis is being conceived (Gerhardt, 2005; Panksepp & Smith Pasqualini, 2005; Stern, 1998; Trevarthen, 2008). The Freudian model of the unconscious mind, "a cauldron of untamed passions and destructive wishes" is being superseded by a more complex picture of the unconscious mind as a "mental structure" (Bucci, 1997; Cimino & Correale, 2005; Davis, 2001; Gergely & Watson, 1996; Ogden, 1992) in which the earliest emotional responses of "how to be with someone" lies at its foundation (Winson, 1990, cited by Schore, 1999, p. 50). It is interesting that this shift in the conceptualisation of the unconscious mind is confirming Darwin's original insight that evolutionary survival rests upon the capacity of the infant to arouse emotions in the mother, and for the mother to aptly respond to these emotional communications.

> The movements of expression in the face and body, whatever their origin may have been, are in themselves of much importance for our welfare. They serve as the first means of communication between the mother and her infant; she smiles approval, and thus encourages her child on the right path, or frowns disapproval. [Darwin, 1872, p. 1256]

The idea that it is an evolutionary necessity to become securely attached if we are to grow into well-functioning human beings helps to explain the painful emotions that are aroused when we see on video the sensitivity of the newborn infant being compromised by an unrewarding environment.

The compromises the infant has to make if the parents or care-takers are threatening leads infants as young as three months to avoid their parents gaze and freeze their bodies (Murray, 1992). At such moments of terror, the infant's body is in what has been termed a highly "dys-regulated" state (Fraiberg, 1982). Winnicott (1958) expressed a similar idea when he spoke of "a freezing of the failure situation" (p. 281). (I am indebted to Patrick Casement for this comment.) What the dysregulated state captures is the profound psychosomatic changes that take place within the infant and its developing brain, if it is left too long in this state. Prolonged distress can lead to a lasting dissociated and dysregulated state of mind. For instance, stress leads to the extra production of cortisol, which, in turn, impairs the immune system and disrupts the capacity of the brain to learn (Gerhardt, 2005; Schore, 2002). This observation has led Panksepp to suggest that an infant who is exposed to too much fear during the earliest development of the brain may develop a tendency in adult life to anxiety disorders or phobias. For attachment theory, this dysregulated state leads to disorganized attachment, or "the disease of non-attachment" (Fraiberg, 1987, p. 13) in which the "dysregulated" mother fails to respond or help her infant in a state of "dysregulation" (Fonagy, Steele, Moran, Steele, & Higgitt, 1991). These insights can provide a fruitful way of thinking about an incapacitating phobia, for instance. If, as is being suggested, the phobia has been an attempt to manage an over-aroused state in early infancy, then we can imagine that what needs to be done in the here and now of a session is to help the patient calm himself down, in the first place, and probably for many sessions (Greenspan, 1997, quoted in Alvarez, 2010).

The idea that the infant needs help with what neurologists are calling dysregulated states within its body is similar to Winnicott's idea of what a "good enough mother" is doing, and meets up with Bion's concept of the "container" mother helping to "contain" her infant's projections of fear and distress (Bion, 1962; Winnicott, 1953). The idea of "not being in our right mind" seems to have been a profound psychological insight that has been confirmed by neurological research. Two thousand years ago, it was written that Jesus cast out the Devil and restored Legion to "his right mind" (Mark, 5: 15, Holy Bible). But neurological research is extending the psychological insights of psychoanalysts such as Winnicott and Bion into a wider or more fundamental framework of what it is to be alive. The picture that is emerging from the neurological studies of earliest infancy is that it is the somatic–affective *interactive* experiences that structure the internal world and hold the clue to psychopathology. The worst terrors of infancy are concerned with the fear of dying, and this fear is precipitated if there is no relationship at hand.

To summarize so far, different strands of research in biology, neurology, and psychology are finding a common ground in their observations of the earliest interactions between mother and child. The infant can only regulate itself through the help of others, but, at the same time, the infant is exquisitely attuned and sensitive to others, which, in turn, stimulates the right brain of the care-taker (Gerhardt, 2005; Panksepp & Smith Pasqualini, 2005; Schore, 2002; Trevarthen, 2008). This, in turn, marries up with the idea that inter-subjectivity and the capacity for empathy develops through the fine-tuning of this earliest relationship. This earliest relationship is internalized and represented, and gives us grounds to believe that psychic structure is created through the intrapsychic states of mind of mother and child in relationship to each other (Jones, 2010).

So, to return to Nicholas, I have found that the work in neurology and the ideas about the developing infant brain have added new ways of thinking about several difficult and confusing moments in the therapy with him. Why was I so inwardly distressed when he told me that he had been put out of earshot so that his cries could not disturb his father? What rendered me speechless when he told me that his father had left when he was six? How could I stretch across the blank hole in his mind?

When Nicholas told me that he was put out of earshot so his parents could not hear his cries, I now believe that the right side of my brain was aroused when I imagined him as an infant in an unbearable state of distress. What was confusing at the time was that I was highly aroused, yet Nicholas was completely cut off from all feeling. This discordance left me bewildered; why was I the one with all the feeling and he appeared indifferent? I felt there was either something unanalysed in me or unanalysable in him. I can now see that my arousal was the appropriate response to an infant in distress, the difficulty was that my arousal met a blank in him. He was warding off the "timeless horror" of not being heard. He had succeeded in arousing me, unlike his mother or father, but it took us both a long time to make manageable and find a language for the emotions that he gradually learnt to bear. The more general reflection I have been left with is that a discordant state, where the therapist feels a strong emotion and the patient is dissociated, might be a powerful communication of infantile trauma (see Cimino & Correale, 2005). If the strength of the discrepancy between these two feeling states is profound, then it may also help to make sense of the length of time a therapy can take. The gap between the early, wordless experience of traumatic dysregulation and the capacity to know and bear the pain might necessitate many hours of constructive suffering between therapist and patient before the pain becomes bearable.

A more confusing experience Nicholas and I both had was over my silence when he told me in a dismissive way that his father had walked out on the family when he was six and he had never seen him since. I was aroused in a very different way this time. I suffered so many competing emotions that I could say nothing, and Nicholas became distressed by my silence. Neurological research has given me a new way of thinking about Nicholas's distress and my silence. As we have seen, the infant needs an attuned mother to help it with the different states of arousal that it experiences, but no mother is ever perfectly attuned and the infant needs to develop the capacity to manage dysregulation as well as attunement (Schore, 2002; Tronick & Cohn, 1989). With someone like Nicholas, whose parents left him alone to manage his distress, he could only turn away and shut off his feelings. As he grew up, he still used these early defences when he felt distress. He would empty out his mind and go blank and then, uncontrollably, he would rage and break things. He had assumed that his rages had no meaning and were the result of what his mother called his "difficult temperament". When I became speechless, he felt again that he had been put out of earshot, and was in a state of what I would now call "dysregulation". I understood the experience at the time as having enacted an early scene from infancy, and while that went some way in helping us to think about what had happened, I did not understand why we needed to go back constantly to this difficulty between us. In fact, we were trying to find a way of managing better that powerful experience of dysregulation. Over time, he gained the confidence to allow him to regulate the frightening moments of dysregulation that inevitably take place between people, and he ceased to rage or empty out his mind.

There was one final difficulty that neurology and attachment theory helped me to understand better. So far, in going back again to the therapy with Nicholas, I have not mentioned the most profound experience that he brought to the therapy. He would have a feeling of bodily disintegration when he sensed I did not understand him. It was similar to the sense of falling into a black hole, or going blank, or what Cohen described as having "a hole in the mind". It was a frightening experience and I was often bewildered as to how to help him manage this experience, especially because he felt it was I who was sending him into this dark and dreadful hole. Now it seems to make sense that this total state of panic can be attributed to the earliest failure of the care-taking environment to help the infant process states of dysregulation. Failure to restore the infant into a well-regulated state eventually means that the whole biological system stops and there follows "the annihilation of one's core being" (Alvarez, 2010). But, at the time of Nicholas's therapy, I did not have this yardstick to help me. We managed as best we could, but, just as I did not have the theoretical help to understand why we had to go over and over the "trauma" of my silence, I did not have the image of an infant in a physical state of over-arousal to help me understand his bodily pain.

Would I do things differently now? Probably not, but I would have been less panicked if I had had the neurological map to help me understand the damage that had been done to Nicholas's psychic structure through the failure of his care-taking environment during the development of the right side of his brain. I believe Nicholas will always be vulnerable to the experience of falling into existential nothingness when he becomes over-stressed, but what I have learnt from working with him, and then from my subsequent reading of the work in attachment theory and neurology, is that the failure of the care-taker to respond to states of distress in the infant mind, during the crucial development of the right side of the brain, can create lasting difficulties in all subsequent relationships.

When Ogden writes that "The early relationship that is of central interest in the analytic setting is not that of mother and infant, but that of the internal object mother and the internal object infant" (Ogden, 1992, p. 203), the research in neurology and attachment theory suggests something more needs to be added. Of course, with our adult patients, we can work only with the relationship they have with us. But what the work of neurological research has helped to bring to life are new imaginative pictures of the way this earliest relationship may be internalized. In the case of Nicholas, I had the unsettling experience of feeling intensely aroused and meeting a blank in his mind. There was no mother there in his mind and there was no relationship for me to catch on to. You might say that I had to create a relationship with him and drag him back into a world where there were people who mattered (Alvarez, 2010).

This leads back to a question raised in the previous chapter. Can "a hole in the mind" be repaired? In the case where a whole community or society has been wiped out, can a lone individual recover from this external devastation? Could such a chaotic experience be got over or mourned in the way suggested by Freud? Krystal's differentiation between adult trauma and infant trauma seemed to suggest, at the very least, that infant trauma is immeasurably more destructive and the neurological research quoted above is now giving a further reason for believing that to be the case.

So, to return to the cases discussed of two great artists, Primo Levi and Arshile Gorky, who survived, respectively, the Jewish and the Armenian genocide; the question had been why in the end did both decide to kill themselves. The answer might now lie with their experiences of the "timeless horror" of earlier infantile trauma, augmented, of course, by their adult traumas. Illness hit them both shortly before their deaths, and perhaps these bodily experiences precipitated them back into the hopeless despair of infancy. They both felt very alone just before they killed themselves: Primo Levi's mother had had a stroke and was an invalid; Gorky's wife had been advised to leave him. Without anyone alongside them in their bodily pain, their infantile experiences of infantile trauma were reawakened and perhaps again they experienced a world that had gone dead. In other words, not only is infantile trauma the worst hell known to man, but neurological research is helping us understand in greater detail just how great is the struggle to repair the original rents in the psychic structure if they have taken place when the right side of the brain is developing in earliest infancy.

So, finally, how might all that has been said add to an understanding of the unconscious transmission of trauma across the generations. It seemed clear that the survivors from the Holocaust carried their traumas within their bodies as well as their psyches. In the cases of those survivors who turned up in psychiatric clinics around the world with their children, it was observed that their adult traumas had interfered with their responses to their children.

Unwittingly, the traumatized parents set up patterns of trauma for their children. The contribution that neurology, biology, and attachment theory is making is that through their different telescopes they are confirming that the earliest patterns of relating or attachment is what becomes internalized and handed on.

Nicholas, if and when he had children, would have been in danger of repeating his early experiences of not knowing how to manage states of emotional dysregulation. His mind would go blank, or, at other times, he would rage uncontrollably. The work we did, I hope, broke that cycle, for, by the end, he had an internal map that could guide him towards distinguishing his different emotions not only within himself, but in other people. This suggests that the cycle of trauma is repeated across the generations through the patterns of child rearing. To break out of this cycle, someone has to intervene. It is vital that a mother who has been badly damaged by trauma is given some help to find a narrative for her suffering, or there will be a danger that she will traumatize her children and the endless cycle of suffering will continue.

In the Preface, I quoted from an uninterpreted dream that a patient had brought me about going to his grandmother's house, with his girl friend, for he knew she would welcome them and give them a meal. This whole book has been about giving a place and a narrative to the unremembered ghosts from family history. It seems to me fitting that I end with another bit of clinical work about an unremembered grandmother. In a talk in 2010 at the Tavistock Clinic, Amanda Jones described her work with a young mother and her baby who was not thriving. Her work follows in the tradition of Fraiberg, and, like Fraiberg, she is sensitive to "the ghosts in the nursery". In the case she presented, and through her sensitive and loving presence with this distressed young girl, the benign ghost of a much loved and forgotten grandmother reappeared. It was the discovery of this grandmother that gave both Jones and her patient hope that this unremembered relationship could once more take its proper place in the internal psychic structure of her granddaughter as she struggled to love and mother her son. In even the grimmest tale of deprivation there might lie a hidden memory of a moment of love or recognition, but, as Faimberg was to say, it needs a relationship with a reliable and concerned other to stir up this forgotten ghost and then give it a history.

REFERENCES

Abraham, N., & Torok, M. (1994). *The Shell and The Kernel*, N. T. Rand (Ed. & Trans.). Chicago, IL: University of Chicago Press.

Abram, J. (2008). Donald Woods Winnicott (1896–1971) a brief introduction. *International Journal of Psychoanalysis, 89*(6): 1189–1217.

Aeschylus (1977). *The Oresteia*, R. Fagles (Trans.). London: Penguin.

Albee, E. (2004). *The Goat, or Who is Sylvia? (Notes Toward a Definition of Tragedy)*. London: Methuen.

Allen, G. (2011). Interview. *Guardian*, 19 January.

Alvarez, A. (2010). Levels of analytic work and levels of pathology. The work of calibration. *International Journal of Psychoanalysis, 91*(4): 859–878.

Angier, C. (2002). *The Double Bond. Primo Levi. A Biography*. New York: Farrar, Straus & Giroux.

Anzieu, D. (1986). *Freud's Self-Analysis*. London: Hogarth.

Balint, E. (1993). *Before I Was I. Psychoanalysis and Imagination*, J. Mitchell & M. Parsons (Eds.). London: Free Association Books.

Barker, P. (1993). *Regeneration*. Harmondsworth: Penguin.

Bateson, G. (1972). *Steps to an Ecology of Mind*. St Albans: Granada Publishing.

Beebe, B., & Lachman, F. (2002). *Infant Research and Adult Treatment. Co-constructing Interactions*. Hillsdale, NJ: Analytic Press.

Bergman, M. S., & Jucovy, M. E. (1982). *Generations of the Holocaust*. New York: Basic Books.

Berlin, I. (1979). *Against the Current. Essays in the History of Ideas*. London: Hogarth Press.

Bion, W. R. (1962). *Learning from Experience*. London: Heinemann Medical.

Bion, W. R. (1982). *The Long Week-End 1897–1919: Part of a Life*. Abingdon: Fleetwood Press.

Bleandonu, G. (1994). *Wilfred Bion. His Life & Works. 1997–1979*. London: Free Association Books.

Blum, H. P. (1969). A psychoanalytic view of *Who's Afraid of Virginia Woolf. Journal of the American Psychoanalytic Association*, 17: 883–903.

Blum, H. P. (1983). Adoptive parents – generative conflict and generational continuity. *Psychoanalytic Study of the Child*, 38: 141–163.

Bollas, C. (2002). *Free Association*. London: Free Association Icon.

Boswell, J. (1988). *The Kindess of Strangers: The Abandonment of Children in Western Europe from Late Antiquity to the Renaissance*. London: Penguin.

Bowlby, J. (1958). *Can I Leave My Baby?* London: National Association for Mental Health.

Bowlby, J. (1969). *Attachment*, Volume 1. Hogarth Press.

Bowlby, R. (2007). *Freudian Mythologies: Greek Tragedies and Modern Identities*. Oxford: Oxford University Press.

Brinich, P. M. (1995). Analytic perspectives on adoption and ambivalence. *Psychoanalytic Psychology*, 12: 181–199.

Brody, S. (1973). The son of a refugee. *Psychoanalytic Study of the Child*, 28: 169–191.

Bucci, W. (1997). Symptoms and symbols. A multiple code theory of symbolisation. *Psychoanalytic Inquiry*, 17: 151–172.

Buergenthal, T. (2010). *A Lucky Child*. London: Profile Books.

Butler, J. (2004). *Precarious Life. The Powers of Mourning & Violence*. London: Verso.

Cohen, J. (1980). Structural consequences of psychic trauma. A new look at *Beyond the Pleasure Principle. International Journal of Psychoanalysis*, 61: 421–423.

Coles, P. (1990). 'How my mother's embroidered apron unfolds in my life': a study on Arshile Gorky. *Free Association*, 20: 49–75.

Coles, P. (2003). *The Importance of Sibling Relationships in Psychoanalysis*. London: Karnac.

Coles, P. (2007). Transgenerational conflicts between sisters. *British Journal of Psychotherapy*, 23(4): 563–575.

Churchill, W. (1930). *My Early Life*. London: Eland, 2002.

Cimino, C., & Correale, A. (2005). Projective identification and consciousness alterations. A bridge between psychoanalysis and neuroscience. *International Journal of Psychoanalysis, 86*(1): 51–60.

Colarusso, C. A. (1987). Mother, is that you? *Psychoanalytic Study of the Child, 42*: 223–237.

Dali, S. (1973). *Comment On Devient Dali: Les Aveux Inavoubles de Salvador Dali*. Paris: R. Laffont.

Danielli, Y. (1984). Psychotherapist participation in the conspiracy of silence about the holocaust. *Psychoanalytic Psychology, 1*: 23–42.

Darwin, C. (1872). The expression of emotion in man. In: J. D. Watson (Ed.), *Darwin. The Indelible Stamp* (pp. 1061–1257). Philadelphia, PA: Running Press.

Davis, J. T. (2001). Revising psychoanalytic interpretations of the past; an examination of declarative and non-declarative memory processes. *International Journal of Psychoanalysis, 82*(3): 449–463.

Davoine, F., & Gaudillière, J.-M. (2004). *A History of Trauma. Whereof One Cannot Speak, Thereof One Cannot Stay Silent*. New York: Other Press.

deMause, L. (Ed.) (1976). *The History of Childhood. The Evolution of Parent–Child Relationships as a Factor in History*. London: Souvenir Press.

Devereux, G. (1953). Why Oedipus killed Laius: a note on the complementary Oedipus complex in Greek drama. *International Journal of Psychoanalysis, 34*: 132–141.

Emery, E. (2002). The ghost in the mother: strange attractors and impossible mourning. *Psychoanalytic Review, 89*: 169–194.

Erikson, E. H. (1955). *Childhood and Society*. London: Vintage.

Faimberg, H. (2005). *The Telescoping of Generations: Listening to the Narcissistic Links between Generations*. London: Routledge.

Feder, L. (1974). Adoption trauma: Oedipus myth/clinical reality. *International Journal of Psychoanalysis, 55*: 491–439.

Field, J. (1934). *A Life of One's Own*. London: Chatto & Windus.

Fildes, V. (1988). *Wet Nursing. A History from Antiquity to the Present*. Oxford: Basil Blackwell.

Fonagy, P., Steele, M., Moran, G., Steele, H., & Higgitt, A. (1991). Measuring the ghost in the nursery: a survey of the main findings of the Anna Freud Centre. UCL parent–child study. *Bulletin of the Anna Freud Centre, 14*: 115–131.

Fraiberg, S. (1982). Pathological defenses in infancy. *Psychoanalytic Quarterly, 51*: 612–635.

Fraiberg, S. (1987). *Selected Writings*, L. Fraiberg (Ed.). Columbus, OH: Ohio State University Press.

Friedman, R. C., & Downey, J. I. (1995). Biology and the Oedipus complex. *Psychoanalytic Quarterly, 64*: 234–264.

Freud, S. (1900a). *Interpretation of Dreams. S.E., 4–5*. London: Hogarth.

Freud, S. (1901b). *The Psychopathology of Everyday Life. S.E., 6*. London: Hogarth.

Freud, S. (1909c). Family romances. *S.E., 9*: 235–242. London: Hogarth.

Freud, S. (1911c). *Psycho-analytic Notes on an Autobiographical Account of Paranoia. S.E., 12*: 3–82. London: Hogarth.

Freud, S. (1915). *The Correspondence of Sigmund Freud to Sandor Ferenczi, Vol 2, 1914–1919*. Harvard University Press, 1996.

Freud, S. (1917b). *A Childhood Reflection from Dichtung und Wahrheit. S.E., 17*: 145–157.

Freud, S. (1917e). Mourning and melancholia. *S.E., 14*: 239–258. London: Hogarth.

Freud, S. (1920g). *Beyond the Pleasure Principle. S.E., 18*: 7–64. London: Hogarth.

Freud, S. (1923b). *The Ego and the Id. S.E., 19*: 3–66. London: Hogarth.

Freud, S. (1933a). *New Introductory Lectures on Psycho-analysis. S.E., 22*: 3–182. London: Hogarth.

Freud, S. (1961). *Letters of Sigmund Freud. 1873–1939*, E. L. Freud (Ed.), T. & J. Stern (Trans.). London: Hogarth Press.

Gathorne-Hardy, J. (1993). *The Rise and Fall of the British Nanny*. London: Weidenfeld & Nicholson.

Gergely, G., & Watson, J. S. (1996). The social bio-feedback theory of parental affect mirroring. *International Journal of Psychoanalysis, 77*(4): 1181–1212.

Gerhardt, S. (2005). *Why Love Matters*. London: Routledge.

Gerson, S. (2009). When the third is dead: memory, mourning and witnessing in the aftermath of the holocaust. *International Journal of Psychoanalysis, 90*(6): 1341–1357.

Ginsburg, L. M. (1999). Sigmund Freud's racial vocabulary and related fragments from the analysis of Clarence P. Oberndorf and Smiley Blanton. *International Forum for Psychoanalysis, 8*: 243–248.

Glasser, M. (1998). On violence. A preliminary communication. *International Journal of Psychoanalysis, 79*(5): 887–902.

Glenn, J. (1974). The adoption theme in Edward Albee's *Tiny Alice* and *The American Dream. Psychoanalytic Study of the Child, 29*: 413–429.

Gonyo, B. (1980). *I'm His Mother, But He is Not my Son*. www.genetic-sexualattraction.com

Green, A. (1983). The Dead Mother. In: *On Private Madness* (pp. 142–174). London: Rebus.

Greenberg, M. (1993). www.geneticsexualattraction.com

Greenspan, S. I. (1997). *Developmentally Based Psychotherapy*. Madison, NY: International Universities Press.

Grosskurth, P. (1985). *Melanie Klein*. London: Maresfield Library.

Grubrich-Simitis, I. (1981). Extreme traumatisation as cumulative trauma: psychoanalytic investigation of the effects of concentration camp experiences on survivors and their children. *Psychoanalytic Study of the Child, 36*: 415–450.

Hardin, H. T. (1985). On the vicissitudes of early primary surrogate mothering. *Journal of the American Psychoanalytic Assocication, 33*: 609–629.

Herzog, J. (1982). A daughter of silence. In: M. S. Bergman & M. E. Jucovy (Eds.), *Generations of the Holocaust*. New York: Basic Books.

Holmes, J. (1993). *John Bowlby and Attachment Theory*. London: Routledge.

Holroyd, M. (2010). *Mosaic*. London: Vintage Books.

Holy Bible. *Old & New Testament. St James*. London: Eyre & Spottiswode Ltd.

Homer (1946). *The Odyssey*, E. V. Rieu (Trans.). London: Penguin Classics.

Hunter, V. (1993). An interview with Hanna Segal. *Psychoanalytic Review, 80*: 1–28.

Jones, A. (2006). Levels of change in parent–infant psychotherapy. *Journal of Child Psychotherapy, 32*(3): 295–311.

Jones, A. (2010). Transference. Confer Conference at the Tavistock Clinic, London, 6 November 2010.

Jucovy, M. E. (1992). Psychoanalytic contributions to holocaust sudies. *International Journal of Psychoanalysis, 73*(2): 267–282.

Kardiner, A. (1977). *My Analysis with Freud: Reminiscences*. New York: Norton.

Kestenberg, J. S. (1972). Psychoanalytic contributions to the problem of children of survivors from the Nazi persecution. *Israel Annals of Psychiatry and Related Disciplines, 10*: 311–325.

Kestenberg, J. S. (1975). *Children & Parents. Psychoanalytic Studies in Development*. New York: Jason Aronson.

Kestenberg, J. S. (1980). Psychoanalysis of children of survivors from the holocaust: case presentation and assessment. *Journal of the American Psychoanalytic Association, 28*: 775–804.

Kestenberg, J. S., & Kestenberg, M. (1982). *Generations of the Holocaust.* New York: Basic Books.

Khan, M. M. R. (1963). The concept of cumulative trauma. *Psychoanalytic Study of the Child, 18*: 286–306.

Klein, M. (1963). Some reflections on the Oresteia. In: *Envy & Gratitude & Other Works, 1946–1963.* New York: Delta Books, 1977.

Kogan, I. (1992). From acting out to words and meaning. *International Journal of Psychoanalysis, 73*(3): 455–467.

Kohon, G. (1999). *The Dead Mother. The Work of André Green,* G. Kohon (Ed.), New York: Routledge, New Library of Psychoanalysis.

Kolin, P. C. (Ed.) (1988). *Conversations with Edward Albee.* Jackson, MI: University of Mississippi Press.

Krystal, H. (1978). Trauma and affects. *Psychoanalytic Study of the Child, 33*: 81–116.

Lacan, J. (1969–1970). *Le Seminaire XVII. L'Envers de la Psychoanalyse.* Paris: Senil, 1991.

Laplanche, J. (1989). *New Foundations for Psychoanalysis,* B. Macey (Trans.). Oxford: Basil Blackwell.

Laplanche, J., & Pontalis, J. B. (1964). Fantasy and the origins of sexuality. *International Journal of Psychoanalysis, 49*: 1–18.

Levi, P. (1958). *If This Is A Man.* London: Abacus, 1987.

Loewald, H. (1980). *Papers on Psychoanalysis.* New Haven, CT: Yale University Press.

Lord, R. (1991). Adoption and identity. A case study. *Psychoanalytic Study of the Child, 46*: 355–367.

Lorenz, K. (1935). *Instructive Behaviour,* C. H. Schiller (Ed.), New York: International Universities Press, 1957.

Mahler, M. (1961). Sadness and grief in childhood. *Psychoanalytic Study of the Child, 16*: 332–351.

Main, M., & Hesse, E. (1990). *Attachment in the Preschool Years. Theory, Research & Intervention,* M. T. Greenberg, D. Chichetti, & E. Cummings (Eds.). Chicago, IL: University of Chicago Press.

Masson, J. M. (Ed.) (1985). *The Complete Letters of Sigmund Freud to Wilhelm Fliess, 1887–1904.* Cambridge, MA: Harvard University Press.

Mitchell, J. (2000). *Mad Men & Medusa. Reclaiming Hysteria and the Effect of Sibling Relations on the Human Condition.* London: Penguin Press.

Morrison, R. (1999). *The Spirit of the Gene.* Ithaca, NY: Cornell University Press.

Murray, L. (1992). The impact of post-natal depression on infant development. *Journal of Child Psychology & Psychiatry, 33*(3): 543–561.

Nickman, S. L. (1985). Losses in adoption. The need for dialogue. *Psychoanalytic Study of the Child, 40*: 365–398.

Niederland, W. G. (1968a). Clinical observations on the 'survivor syndrome'. *International Journal of Psychoanalysis, 49*: 313–315.

Oberndorf, C. P. (1958). *An Autobiographical Sketch.* New York: Cornell University Infirmary & Clinic.

Ogden, T. (1992). *The Primitive Edge of Experience.* London: Karnac.

Ogden, T. (2006). Foreword. In: *The Soul, The Mind, and the Psychoanalyst* (pp. xiii). London: Karnac.

Oliner, M. M. (1982). Hysterical features among children of survivors. In: M. S. Bergman & M. E. Jucovy (Eds.), *Generations of the Holocaust* (pp. 267–287). New York: Basic Books.

Panksepp, J., & Smith Pasqualini, M. (2005). The search for the fundamental brain/mind sources of affective experience. In: J. Nadel & D. Muir (Eds.), *Emotional Development.* Oxford University Press.

Perelberg, R. J. (2009). Murdered father; dead father: revisiting the 'Oedipus complex'. *International Journal of Psychoanalysis, 90*(4): 713–732.

Pollock, G. H. (1961). Mourning and adoption. *International Journal of Psychoanalysis, 42*: 341–361.

Raphael-Leff, J. (1990). If Oedipus was an Eygptian. *International Review of Psychoanalysis, 17*(3): 309–337.

Reiff, P. (1963). The meaning of history and religion in Freud. In: B. Mazlish (Ed.), *Psychoanalysis and History* (p. 25). Englewood Cliffs, NJ: Prentice Hall.

Robertson, P. (1976). Home as a nest: middle class childhood in nineteenth century Europe. In: L. deMause (Ed.), *The History of Childhood* (pp. 407–432). London: Souvenir.

Rocamora, C. (2007). Who am I? *Guardian,* 10 March.

Rosenfeld, D. (2006). *The Soul, The Mind, and The Psychoanalyst. The Creation of the Psychoanalytic Setting in Patients with Psychotic Aspects.* London: Karnac.

Ross, J. M. (1982). Oedipus revisited: Laius and the "Laius complex". *Psychoanalytic Study of the Child, 37*: 169–200.

Sandler, J., Dreher, A. D., & Drews, S. (1991). An approach to conceptual research in psychoanalysis. Illustrated by a consideration of psychic trauma. *International Review of Psychoanalysis, 18*(2): 133–143.

Schore, A. N. (1999). Commentary by Allan N. Schore. *Neuropsychoanalysis, 1*: 49–55.

Schore, A. N. (2002). Advances in neuropsychoanalysis, attachment theory, and trauma research: implications for self psychology. *Psychoanalytic Inquiry, 22*: 433–484.

Schreber, D. P. (1903). *Memoirs of My Mental Illness*. London: Dawson, 1955.

Schützenberger, A. A. (1998). *The Ancestor Syndrome*, A. Trager (Trans.). London: Routledge.

Shakespeare, W. (1966)[1623]. *Two Gentlemen of Verona*. London: Oxford University Press.

Shakespeare, W. (1994)[1599]. *Romeo and Juliet*. Penguin Popular Classics.

Shengold, L. L. (1988). *A Halo in the Sky*. New York: Guilford Press.

Shengold, L. L. (2000). Soul murder reconsidered: "did it really happen?" *Canadian Journal of Psychoanalysis, 8*: 1–18.

Sherick, I. (1983). Adoption and disturbed narcissism: a case illustration of a latency boy. *Journal of the American Psychoanalytic Association, 31*: 487–513.

Siegel, A. M., & Siegel, R. N. (2001). Adoption and the enduring fantasy of an idealized other: progress in self. *Psychology, 17*: 129–147.

Simon, B. (1988). *Psychoanalytic Studies from Aeschylus to Beckett*. New Haven, CT: Yale University Press.

Sophocles (1962). *Oedipus the King*, H. D. F. Kitto (Trans.). Oxford: Oxford University Press.

Steiner, J. (1985). Turning a blind eye: the cover up for Oedipus. *International Review of Psychoanalysis, 12*(2): 161–173.

Stern, D. N. (1985). *The Interpersonal World of the Child. A View from Psychoanalysis and Developmental Psychology*. Basic Books.

Stern, D. N. (1998). Non-interpretative mechanisms in psychoanalytic therapy; the 'something more' than interpretation. *International Journal of Psychoanalysis, 79*(5): 903–921.

Tomlin, C. (1997). *Jane Austen: A Life*. London: Viking.

Trevarthen, C. (2008). Thought in motion. Interdisciplinary approaches to mind and body. Lecture at Tavistock Centre, 5–6 September. New York: Analytic Press.

Tronick, E., & Cohn, J. (1989). Infant–mother face-to-face interaction. Age and gender differences in co-ordination and occurrence of misco-ordination. *Child Development, 60*: 85–92.

Van Dijken, S. (1998). *John Bowlby: His Early Life: A Biographical Journey into the Roots of Attachment Theory*. London: Free Association Books.

Vellacott, P. (1956). *Aeschylus: The Oresteian Trilogy*. London: Penguin Classics.

Vellacott, P. (1971). *Sophocles and Oedipus*. University of Michigan Press.

Vernant, J.-P., & Vidal-Naquet, P. (1972). *Mythe et tragédie en Grèce ancienne* (Volumes 1 and 2). Paris: La Deconverte/Poche, 2001.

Wagonfeld, S., & Emde, R. N. (1982). Anaclitic depression—a follow-up from infancy to puberty. *Psychoanalytic Study of the Child, 37*: 67–94.

Watling, E. F. (1947). *Sophocles: The Theban Plays*. London: Penguin Classics.

Welldon, E. (1992). *Mother, Madonna, Whore. The Idealization and Denigration of Motherhood*. London: Karnac.

Wieder, H. (1977). The family romance fantasies of adopted children. *Psychoanalytic Quarterly, 46*: 185–200.

Wiesel, E. (1970). *Legends of our Time*. Bristol: Avon Books.

Winnick, H. Z. (1968). Contribution to symposium on psychic traumatization through social catastrophe. *International Journal of Psychoanalysis, 49*: 298–301.

Winnicott, D. W. (1953). Transitional objects and transitional phenomena. *International Journal of Psychoanalysis, 34*: 89–97.

Winnicott, D. W. (1958). *Collected Papers. Through Pediatrics to Psychoanalysis*. London: Tavistock Publications.

Winnicott, D. W. (1971). *Playing and Reality*. London: Tavistock.

Winson, J. (1990). The meaning of dreams. *Scientific American*, November: 86–96.

Wittgenstein, L. (1914). Notes on logic. Appendix I of *Notebooks 1914–1916* (2nd edn), G. H. von Wright and G. E. M. Anscombe (Eds.). Oxford: Basil Blackwell, 1979.

Wittgenstein, L. (1918). *Tractatus Logico-Philosophy*. London: Dover, 1999.

Wittgenstein, L. (1933–1934). *Blue & Brown Books*. Oxford: Harper Torchbooks, 1965.

Young-Bruehl, E. (1989). Looking for Anna Freud's mother. *Psychoanalytic Study of the Child, 44*: 391–408.

Zetzel, E. (1970). Discussion of 'Towards a basic psychoanalytic model'. *International Journal of Psychoanalysis, 51*: 183–193.

INDEX